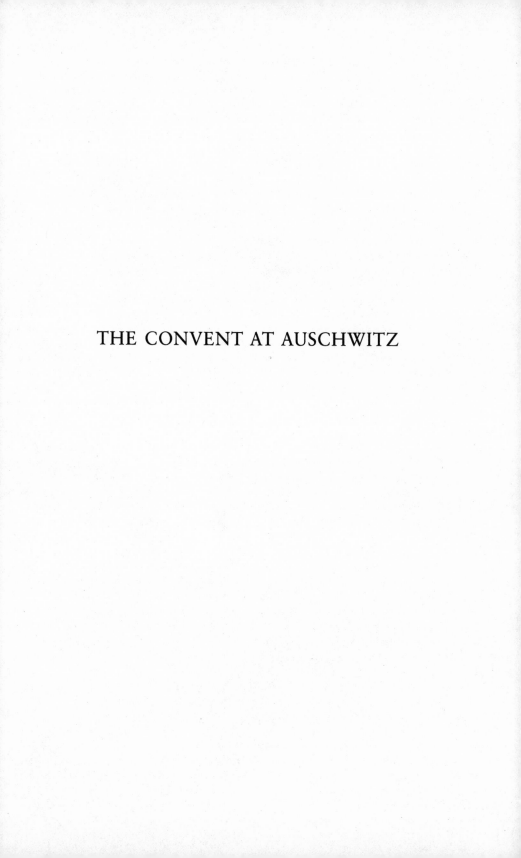

THE CONVENT AT AUSCHWITZ

THE CONVENT

AT

AUSCHWITZ

WLADYSLAW T. BARTOSZEWSKI

GEORGE BRAZILLER

NEW YORK

First published in the United States in 1991 by George Braziller, Inc.
Published in Great Britain in 1990 by Bowerdean Press Ltd.
Copyright © 1990 by Wladyslaw T. Bartoszewski
All rights reserved.
For information, write to the publisher:

George Braziller, Inc.
60 Madison Avenue
New York, New York 10010

Library of Congress Cataloging-in-Publication Data

Bartoszewski, Wladyslaw.
    The convent at Auschwitz / Wladyslaw T. Bartoszewski.
      p.   cm.
    ISBN 0–8076–1267–7 : $17.95
    1. Carmelite Nuns—Poland—Oświęcim.   2. Auschwitz (Poland :
Concentration camp)   3. Christianity and other religions—
Judaism—1945–   4. Judaism—Relations—Christianity—1945–
5. Judaism—Relations—Catholic Church.   6. Catholic Church—
Relations—Judaism.   7. Poland—Ethnic relations.   8. Poland—
Church history—20th century.   9. Oświęcim (Poland)—Church
history.   I. Title.
BX4324.088B37   1990
261.2'6'094385—dc20   91–10127
                                                     CIP

Manufactured in the United States of America.

First U.S. Edition

Contents

To Andrew S. Ciechanowiecki, an archetypal Maecenas, whose tireless devotion to culture has helped so many.

Acknowledgments

I am grateful to many people for their help in the preparation of this book. I would like to thank the Annenberg Research Institute and its director, Bernard Lewis, my father Władysław Bartoszewski, Fr Adam Boniecki, MIC, Harvey Goldberg, Ronald Modras, Alexandra Reiche, Keith Sword, Rabbi Marc H. Tanenbaum, Jonathan Webber and Stefan Wilkanowicz. A special word of thanks goes to Antony Polonsky for his continuous support and encouragement. They are not responsible, however, for the views expressed in the book.

Finally, I would like to thank Anna Zaranko who provided me with great support as editor, translator and critic and who made it all possible.

The map of the Auschwitz region is reproduced by kind permission of Martin Gilbert.

THE AUSCHWITZ REGION

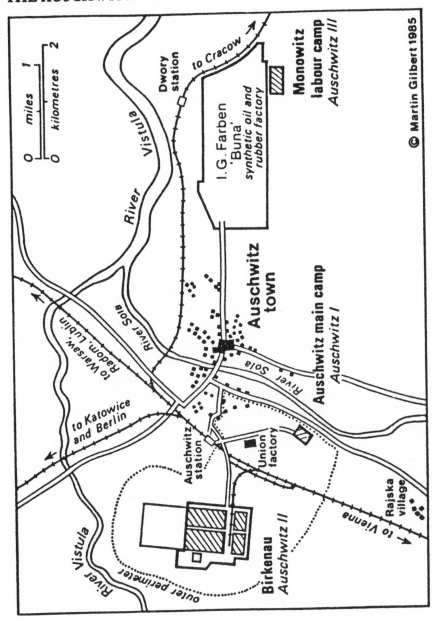

© Martin Gilbert 1985

Auschwitz 1

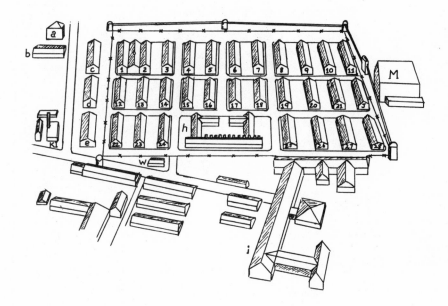

MAP KEY

1–28 Inmates' barracks
a) Commandant's house
b) Main guardhouse
c) Commandant's office
d) Administration Building
e) Hospital for the SS
KI Gas chamber and crematorium
W) Guardhouse at camp entrance
h) Kitchen
i) Arrival/reception area
M) Old Theatre, then storehouse for valuables removed from bodies,
    site of the carmelite Convent
J) New laundry house

THE CONVENT AT AUSCHWITZ

CHAPTER 1

Introduction

Polish-Jewish relations go back to the 10th century when the first Jewish communities appeared in the country. Poland lay between western and eastern markets and well-travelled trade routes soon developed across the country's plains. There was also considerable Arabian trade with northern and eastern Europe. The role of the Jews grew with the introduction of monetary trade. Soon there were Jews in charge of the mints producing coins bearing the Polish sovereign's name in Hebrew letters. Between the 10th and the 13th century the everyday language of the Jews was Slavonic, which was only later overtaken by Yiddish. The big development of the community occurred in the 13th century during the great migration wave from western Europe. Faced with growing religious intolerance and expulsion, which began during the Crusades and intensified in the 13th century, Jews began to move eastwards in large numbers.

In 1264, Boleslaus the Pious granted the Jews a privilege known as the Kalisz Statute. This, and the later Extended Privilege, became the two main documents regulating the Jewish legal and social position in Poland until the 18th century. The privileges ensured the personal protection of the Jews, their property, and religion. It allowed them to organise their communities according to principles of self-government, and to engage freely in trade and money-lending. Their main occupation for the next couple of centuries was trade. Many of them leased property, including the royal mint and salt mines, and collected customs and tolls. Few of them were engaged in agriculture, although some owned villages, manors, fish ponds and mills.

In the later Middle Ages, Jewish economic activity expanded to encompass fur-making, tailoring, tanning, and other crafts – all of which aroused the opposition of the Christian burghers. In the 14th and 15th centuries there were anti-Jewish riots in various cities as a result.

The 16th century witnessed a flood of immigrants as a result of widespread persecution and expulsions from Eastern Germany. The

1

Jewish population increased to constitute five per cent of the overall population. The Polish rulers welcomed this influx which they considered to be beneficial to the country's economy and granted the Jews a variety of privileges. Even Spanish and Portuguese Jews found their way to Polish cities, despite the local resistance of burghers who feared Jewish competition and obtained privileges *de non tolerandis Judaeis* which forbade the Jews to reside in some towns. The result was often segregation of the Jews in separate quarters, or their settlement just outside the city walls, which were under the rule of the nobility and the Church.

The later centuries were characterised by the constant struggle between the townspeople and the Jews. The latter were often supported by the kings and the nobility who drew considerable benefits from the Jewish presence. The nobility was by law forbidden to trade (with the exception of grain and timber) and therefore relied largely on Jewish craftsmen and tradesmen residing on their estates. The Jews were also engaged in managing noble estates, and in toll and tax farming.

The Jews who, unlike the burghers, did not compete with the nobility politically, operated in a sense outside the estate structure. They were not tied to the land like peasants. They did not have many of the rights enjoyed by the townsmen (as a result of the above-mentioned laws). On the other hand, they enjoyed self-governing autonomy under their own diet (between 1581 and 1764) and from 1588 were automatically ennobled if they embraced Christianity.[1] During that time Polish Jews enjoyed more autonomy than anywhere else in Europe. Community elders took care of all internal matters, be they economic, legal, cultural or religious, and the Diet, the Council of the Four Lands, represented all the Jews in their relations with the Polish state. From the point of view of the monarch, the Council's most important function was to organise and collect the poll-tax from Polish Jews.

Between the 16th and 18th centuries, the Jews entered into what may be described as a marriage of convenience with the nobility. As a result of the legal protection enjoyed by the Polish Jews, their economic co-operation with the magnates and their autonomy within the state, 16th and 17th century Poland was described as 'heaven for the Jews, paradise for the nobles, hell for the serfs'.

The Jewish community suffered greatly during the 1648 Cossack uprising which had been directed primarily against the Polish nobility. The Jews, perceived as allies of the nobles, were also victims of the revolt, during which about twenty per cent of them were killed.

The second half of the 17th and the 18th century brought a significant deterioration in the Jewish situation. Constant wars fought on Polish soil led to the pauperization of towns and practically paralysed all long distance and foreign trade. During that period many Jews became travelling craftsmen and petty traders, the so-called peddlars, who moved between small towns and villages selling small items to the peasants and repairing things on the spot. They became indispensable to the rural economy as tailors, shoemakers, carpenters, haberdashers, blacksmiths etc. The interdependence between Polish village and small Jewish town (*shtetl*) which was unique in Europe persisted until 1939.

In the 18th century Poland lost its independence following three partitions by Russia, Prussia, and Austria, in 1772, 1793 and 1795. Polish Jews became subjects of foreign monarchs, some of whom – like Catherine the Great – had not previously ruled over Jews. They determined the legal position of the Jews until 1918, when Poland regained independence.

During the 19th century Jews ceased to be a feudal estate and gained civil rights (in Prussia in 1850, in Austria in 1867–8, partially in Russia in 1862). Their relations with the Poles were largely linked to the question of Polish independence. The Jews participated in two armed uprisings against the Tsars in 1830–31 and 1863–64. The second half of the century witnessed an industrial revolution and the breakdown of traditional rural society. This resulted in the creation of a Jewish middle-class which was first glorified by the Poles as a harbinger of economic progress, but was soon criticised on the grounds that capitalism went against their traditional value-system. Any sign of Jewish co-operation with the (foreign) authorities was considered by the Poles to be detrimental to the central issue of independence and was regarded as unpatriotic. The accusation of lack of patriotism has been a constant one throughout the 20th century and was to intensify with the emergence of the concept of a communist-Jewish alliance, commonly referred to as 'Judeo-Communism'.

The Jews perceived the Poles in an equally stereotypical way. In early modern times the Jews considered all other nations to have been created for their benefit – 'were it not that there is some good [that comes from them] they would not have been created at all' – preached Rabbi Levi Yitshak of Berdichev to his followers at the end of the 18th century.[2] In the 19th century this image was enriched by some new elements according to which all Gentiles could be divided into revolutionary philo-semites and reactionary anti-semites. The transformation of the country from the feudal system of complementary estates to the modern world was characterised by the growth of nationalism, industrial development, and economic competition. The difficult adaptation to the new socio-economic structure raised a variety of problems including the acculturation, assimilation and secularisation of the Jews. The newly emerging national identities put great strain on Polish-Jewish relations. The new Polish and Jewish political parties fought the prolonged battle with each other which continued until the outbreak of the Second World War. Polish nationalism and especially the National Democratic Party of Roman Dmowski had a dramatic and adverse effect on Jewish life in Poland, and modern political anti-semitism established itself as a significant force.

The traditional Jewish responses to the Gentile world: the fight for civil rights, emancipation and assimilation, proved ineffective. The anti-Jewish policies of Tsar Alexander III, largely continued by his successor Nicholas II (under whom most of Polish Jewry lived, since they inhabited the area of Poland incorporated into Russia during the partitions), prompted the emergence of Zionism and Jewish socialism, represented by the Bund, and the mass emigration to the United States and Western Europe.

After the re-creation of the Polish Republic in 1918 its Jewish community was still the largest in Europe, constituting approximately ten per cent of the Polish population. Most of them lived in the cities although almost a quarter lived in villages, which allowed for the continuation of the unique *shtetl* communities. The overwhelming majority of Jews worked in commerce, industry, and the professions and in some areas the Jews constituted a majority. Tailoring and shoemaking were typical Jewish occupations, as was shopkeeping. At the same time 56 per cent of all doctors, 43 per cent of teachers, 33 per cent of lawyers, and 22 per cent of journalists were Jewish. Most Jews belonged to the petty-bourgeoisie and were not well off.[3] Depressed economic conditions and anti-semitism, which was rampant in Poland especially between 1918–1923 and 1936–38 forced many Jews to emigrate. As Ezra Mendelsohn stated 'The experience of Polish Jews between the wars was a combination of suffering, some of which was caused by anti-semitism, and of achievement made possible by Polish freedom, pluralism, and tolerance.'⁴ Despite the anti-semitism, Jewish politics, culture, and religion flourished and made for a spiritually rich and varied life. Jewish education and scholarship prospered. The press was in three languages (Yiddish, Hebrew and Polish). Social, communal, political and religious organisations blossomed in a way which made autonomous Jewish life in Poland richer and more interesting than that in Western Europe and America.

Almost 40 per cent of the pre-war Polish population belonged to ethnic minorities (apart from the Jews there were Ukrainians, Byelorussians, Germans, and others). After some hesitation the Polish government opted for the 'nation state' instead of a 'state of nationalities' which made the lives of minorities more difficult.

Almost the entire three and a half million strong Jewish population perished during the Second World War. There are no accurate figures about the number of survivors but it is estimated that only 100,000 of them remained in Poland by 1945. The majority of those left soon after because they did not want to live on amongst the ashes of the community, because they feared Communist power, and because they were shocked by the anti-semitic violence which swept the country in 1946, (especially after the Kielce pogrom, in July 1946, during which 42 Jews were killed).

CHAPTER 2

Origins

The Origins of the Controversy

In May 1985, Pope John Paul II visited Belgium. The head of a charitable Catholic organisation, *Aide à l'Eglise en détresse*, Father Wilfried van Straaten, conceived the idea of welcoming the Pontiff with a gift. Since the organisation specialised in helping the churches behind the Iron Curtain, and considering the national origin of the Pope, van Straaten felt it appropriate to provide financial support for the Polish religious community which had already benefitted from such support in the past. A suitable beneficiary was easily found. In 1984, a few Discalced* Carmelite nuns obtained permission to establish a convent at Auschwitz. In the autumn of 1984 they moved to a derelict building, which bordered on the site of the Nazi concentration camp. The building, which was constructed just before the First World War by the Austro-Hungarian Empire, was meant to be a theatre to entertain the troops living in the nearby barracks. The outbreak of the First World War had prevented the building from ever being used for its original purpose. The place became notorious only much later, during the Second World War: from 1940 the old barracks housed Polish political prisoners and soon became known as Auschwitz concentration camp. The theatre building itself was used as a storage house by the Nazis.

When the building was handed over to the nuns, the site was derelict and lacked all basic amenities. In order to convert it into a convent the nuns needed considerable financial assistance which was not available in Poland. The Belgian organisation, whose headquarters were based in West Germany, decided that the convent would be the most appropriate recipient of their charity, especially considering the Pope's interest in Auschwitz which he described in his sermon delivered there on 7 June 1979 as a place '... built for the

* See Chapter 3 note 2.

6

negation of faith – faith in God and faith in man – and to trample in a thorough-going way not only on love but on all signs of human dignity, of humanity'. The Pope also mentioned the martyrdom of Catholics at Auschwitz during the war and stated that they achieved redemption through it. The Pontiff recalled two martyrs for the faith who perished in the camp, Father Maximilian Kolbe who was subsequently canonized, and a Carmelite sister, Edith Stein, who was a converted Jewess, blessed in 1987. These remarks were to become an inspiration and justification for the presence of Carmelite nuns in the camp.[1]

Aide à l'Eglise en détresse began an energetic fund-raising campaign in support of the nuns to coincide with the Pope's visit to Benelux. The text of the appeal which had not been discussed with the Carmelites or with the Polish ecclesiastical authorities, contained phrases which sparked off the controversy which has been raging ever since. The newsletter of the Belgian organisation appealed to its supporters to give donations:

> After the Pope's visit, we wish to present him as a gift from our benefactors in the Benelux countries the sum of money necessary to found the convent, which will become a spiritual fortress and a guarantee of the conversion of strayed brothers from our countries as well as proof of our desire to erase the outrages so often done to the Vicar of Christ.

This appeal came to the attention of Jewish circles in Belgium who expressed their unease about the Catholic presence at the camp. To assuage these fears and to explain Catholic aims, Michel Bailly published an article on 14 October 1985 in the Brussels Journal *Le Soir* entitled 'The Carmelite Convent in the Depository of Deathly Gas in Auschwitz'. The article attempted to reassure the Jews that the creation of a new convent was not a provocation, and that any intention to diminish 'the immense sacrifice suffered by the Jews and the permanence of their enormous, tragic witness' would be deplorable. The article also repeated parts of the appeal made by the Church in Distress. It was these phrases which aroused most objections from the Jewish community. A wave of protests followed, provoked particularly by the expression 'conversion of strayed brothers' and the reference to 'the outrages so often done to the Vicar of Christ'. The conversion was understood to have meant that the nuns would not only pray for the conversion of the Jews, but would also 'convert' the Jewish victims of Auschwitz-Birkenau camps. The Pope's mention of Father Maximilian Kolbe and the Carmelite sister Edith Stein were considered to be especially provocative because although no one questioned Kolbe's bravery in the camp (he sacrificed his life in order to save that of a man with a family who indeed survived the camp), he was nevertheless the editor of an anti-semitic paper before the war, while Edith Stein was a converted Jewess and was thus perceived to have died because of her ethnic origin rather than as a martyr for the Catholic faith. The reference to the Vicar of Christ was interpreted as an attempt to combat the often-repeated accusations against Pope Pius XII, who was considered to have done very little to try to save the Jews from the Nazis. In reality it appears that Father van Straaten had primarily objected to the attacks on Pope John Paul II emanating from the Dutch Catholics, who disagreed with various aspects of the Vatican's teaching on such issues as abortion, homosexuality, celibacy of the clergy and women priests.

Generally, the language of the appeal was considered to be offensive, triumphalist, and militant, suggesting a kind of new religious crusade against the Jews. The controversy, which was at first limited to the French-language community, quickly spread to involve Jewish communities throughout Western Europe and the USA. Their reaction was to call for the removal of the convent since its purpose was felt to be to de-Judaize the Holocaust. As Markus Pardes, President of the Coordinating Committee of Jewish Organisations in Belgium, stated 'we want to keep Auschwitz as an eternal memorial to the Holocaust of the Jews.'[23]

The Belgian Jewish community met in February of 1986 with Cardinal Franciszek Macharski, Archbishop of Cracow, in whose diocese Auschwitz is located. During the meeting the Jewish leaders outlined the reasons for their opposition to the Carmelite presence in the camp. The convent was considered to be an insult to the Jewish people because Auschwitz is for them the main symbol of the Holocaust. The Catholic religious presence would help to obliterate the memory of the Jewish sacrifice and 'accelerate the banalization' of the tragedy. The Jews pointed out that the unilateral action was contrary to the spirit of dialogue in which Christian and Jewish communities had been engaged since the Second Vatican Council, and that since 'the founding of the convent was to be a reflection of the Catholic Church's sense of duty towards the Holocaust victims, it should be done in a way which did not offend those very people it was aimed at.'

Cardinal Macharski, while recognising that Jews were the principal victims of the camp, considered Auschwitz to be a symbol of evil for all humanity, for Poles and Jews alike. He believed that 'the convent was a concrete manifestation of a desire to pray and repent'.

The essence of the controversy which has raged since then has to do precisely with these two different interpretations of the symbolic nature of the Auschwitz camp.

Auschwitz in Polish Memory

The Poles do not regard Auschwitz as a specifically 'Jewish' camp. It was opened in June 1940 as a concentration camp for Polish political prisoners. Its origins go back to 28 September 1939, when Hitler and Stalin signed the Boundary and Friendship Treaty which contained secret provisions for the mutual extermination of potential Polish opponents of both regimes. Both the Soviet Union and Germany were to take all the necessary steps to contain and prevent the emergence of any hostile campaign directed against the territory of the other side. They would crush any signs of agitation within their own territories and inform each other of means employed to achieve this aim. The Soviet side implemented their part of the agreement by executing almost 15,000 Polish POWs, 45 per cent of the pre-war Polish officer corps, in the Katyn forest near Smolensk and in other still unknown locations in April/May 1940. On the Nazi side, at the end of April 1940 Heinrich Himmler ordered the removal of 20,000 Poles to concentration camps. In May the *Aktion AB* (*Ausserordentliche Befriedungsaktion*) began – a grand design to exterminate the Polish intelligentsia within German-occupied Poland. According to the SS, the campaign was meant to entrap 'the spiritual and political leaders of the Polish resistance movement'.[4] On 14 June 1940, the first transport of Polish prisoners arrived in Auschwitz, which for the next 21 months was to be inhabited almost exclusively by Poles.

The decision to set up the camp was taken because it was the most practical way to carry out the destruction of the Polish elite close to where they lived. At the same time, Auschwitz was situated on that part of pre-war Polish territory which had been incorporated into the Third Reich. Its establishment was preceded by large-scale resettlement of the local population of the entire district which left no Poles in the vicinity. This was done in order to isolate the future inmates and to ensure that they would not be provided with any assistance. The term 'elite' has to be understood in the widest poss-

9

ible sense because it included anybody with a secondary education. In fact, the first transports to the camp brought a few thousand Polish men between the ages of 18 and 65 who were rounded up in the course of raids in streets and houses in Warsaw and elsewhere. In the summer of 1941, the first foreigners coming from Bohemia arrived in the camp, followed shortly after by thousands of Soviet prisoners of war. The first Jews, 999 women from Slovakia, did not reach the camp until 26 March 1942.[5]

In the collective memory of the Poles, Auschwitz is primarily the camp set up to destroy the most prominent elements of the Polish nation, 270,000 of whom perished there.

The Jewish prisoners of Auschwitz accounted for 14 per cent of the inmates. The Poles thus deny the Jewish claim to exclusivity, since the Poles were always in the majority in the main camp. This memory does not encompass the sub-camp at Birkenau referred to also as Auschwitz II, where millions of Jews were killed together with some Russians, Poles, Czechs, Frenchmen, and Gypsies, but where the victims were 90 per cent Jewish. The Jews therefore regard the Auschwitz-Birkenau complex as the biggest Jewish cemetery in history. For this reason, the camp has acquired a symbolic value or meaning quite different from that which it has for the Poles. Indeed, some Jews are surprised or outraged to learn that Auschwitz was not originally set up solely in order to exterminate their nation and that the Polish victims of the camp were so numerous. This applies even in the case of some well established professional historians. Pierre Vidal-Naquet in his contribution to the debate published in Belgium by the periodical *Regards* which was largely responsible for bringing the issue to the attention of a wider public, stated that it is 'incredible' that one Polish historian claimed that 'Auschwitz was created primarily for the extermination of the Poles and only subsequently of the Jews'.[6] Yet the claim is correct, especially in respect of the elite of the Polish nation. Suprisingly, Vidal-Naquet had made this criticism in a much more appropriate form a few years previously in his essay 'A Paper Eichmann' (1980) in which he objected – absolutely rightly – to the claim made by the same Polish historian that 'the Slavs, and particularly the Poles and the Russians were the main victims of the biological extermination in Auschwitz-Birkenau'.[7] This is indeed one of the distinctions which both Poles and Jews often fail to make. Although Auschwitz I was created in June 1940 in order to facilitate the murder of the Polish elite whose members were for a year the only inmates of the camp (they were joined in June

1941 by some Czechs and later by the representatives of 29 other nationalities), it was in May 1942 when the newly constructed Auschwitz II (Birkenau) begun to operate that the nature of the place changed from a concentration to a death (extermination) camp. This is a fact which the Poles do not take into account: the treatment of Jews after the creation of a sub-camp at Birkenau was not comparable with that which faced the Poles earlier. There were, after all, no gas chambers for the Poles. The first victims of the gas chambers were, in September 1941, 600 Soviet prisoners-of-war and 250 prisoners suffering from consumption. The success of this experimental gassing, conducted in a specially constructed bunker in the main camp, convinced the Nazis to use Cyklon B on a wider scale on the Jews who were, from the summer of 1941 onwards, expected to appear in the camp. The SS decided in October 1941 to build a sub-camp in Birkenau, about two miles away, for another 200,000 prisoners. The main gas chambers were located in the new camp; the first was built in the late Autumn of 1941, the second in June 1942, followed by more in March 1943. From May 1942 the majority of the Jews arriving in Auschwitz-Birkenau were sent straight from the railway ramp to the gas chambers. No other national group was so treated. There is no agreement about the number of Jewish victims of the camp. The estimates have varied from 1.35 million to four million people (the former is still supported for example by Yehuda Bauer, one of the most senior Holocaust scholars; the latter is now rejected by most historians), while the real figure, although impossible to establish precisely, was probably around 1.5 million Jews.[8]

At the same time Vidal-Naquet stated openly that: 'As a Jew I have to say that Jewish historiography has a tendency to take only what happened to the Jews into account and neglect what the others were subjected to'.[9] The official Polish historiography, controlled as it was until recently by the party line of the Communists, took a precisely opposite view negating the Jewishness of the victims. When volume eight of the Great Popular Encyclopedia appeared in 1966 in Poland, it contained an entry on the Nazi concentration camps. In it the reader could find a straightforward and quite reliable description of Nazi policy and the camps. Two years later, during the virulent anti-semitic campaign conducted especially by the Polish (but also by other) communist governments after the Six-Day war between Israel and the Arab states, this entry was severely criticised by the party ideologues. The publisher was forced to print an amended description of the camps, which was sent in the form of a four-page leaflet to all the subscribers of the Encyclopedia. The corrected entry negated the distinction between the concentration camps (where the majority of the inmates were always Polish), and the death camps (whose millions of victims were almost entirely Jewish). The martyrdom of the Polish nation was emphasised and that of the Jews played down. The reason for this change, according to the authorities, was the falsification of the history of the camps perpetrated by capitalist publications (including the encyclopedias) and the 'the tragic, in its political significance, alliance between Israel and West Germany'.[10] It is true that this action, taken by the Polish government of Władysław Gomułka, still fell short of that taken by the Soviet government after the fall of Lavrenti Beria. The Soviet subscribers to the Great Soviet Encyclopedia were then asked to cut out the entry for 'Beria' which was then to be replaced by a new one. When the new entries arrived the subscribers noticed that the new text was devoted entirely to a long discussion of the Barents Sea ... The principle of re-writing history, much favoured by various rulers throughout history and a common practice for the twentieth-century communists, has frequently affected Jewish themes also.

The Jewish Memory of Auschwitz

It is a matter for speculation as to why Auschwitz in particular became a universal symbol of the Holocaust for the Jewish community, apart from the sheer number of its victims. Auschwitz-Birkenau was not the first, and in some respects not even the most terrifying of the Nazi extermination camps. The first such camp was Chełmno (Kulmhof) where the killing of Jews began on 8 December 1941, before the plans for the implementation of the 'Final Solution of the Jewish question' were finalized at a conference which took place in a Berlin suburb, Wansee, on 20 January 1942. Chełmno was followed in March 1942 by the camp at Bełżec and in April of that year by the one in Sobibór. On 23 July 1942, the killing began in the Treblinka camp. These four camps together claimed more Jewish victims than Auschwitz and the number of survivors was minimal. Martin Gilbert estimated that Chełmno destroyed 360,000 Jews, of which only three survived. The respective figures for Bełżec were 600,000 killed and two survivors. As a result of the uprising by the inmates of Sobibór, followed by a mass escape of prisoners, 64 people survived the camp while 250,000 perished. For the same reason Treblinka, possibly the most horrifying death machine ever built, claiming 870,000 Jews, was survived by between 40 and 70 people.[11]

Thus the thousands of Jews who survived Auschwitz contributed to the emergence of the camp as the main symbol of the destruction of the Jewish nation. This comparatively high survival rate was due to the fact that a considerable number of Jews arriving in Auschwitz were selected for slave labour and not murdered outright as in other camps. Another potential factor was the international character of Auschwitz. The majority of Polish Jewry died in the four above-mentioned death camps – Bełżec, Treblinka, Sobibór, and Chełmno. Auschwitz became the grave of European Jewry. Therefore, for the Jews of Warsaw, which was the biggest Jewish urban centre in Europe, it is Treblinka, the most efficient killing machine – from the operational point of view, the most 'perfect' camp – which is of greater symbolic significance, since almost all the Jews in Warsaw perished there. For the international Jewish community, however, it is Auschwitz which has continued to be a symbol even though the overwhelming majority of the six million Jews who were murdered during the war died elsewhere. Lastly, it has been suggested that the fact that the old buildings of the camp still exist and can be visited has played an important role in the creation of Auschwitz as *the* symbol of the destruction of the Jews. There are no traces of the other death camps left, the remains having been deliberately destroyed by the Nazis. In Treblinka, for example, there is a symbolic cemetery made of stones, each of which represents a particular Jewish community whose members perished there. It forms a moving monument to the victims of the camp, but no trace of the original camp itself is to be found. In 1943 after Treblinka had largely been destroyed by a fire started during the rebellion of the inmates the camp was dismantled, the bricks of the gas chambers used to construct a farmhouse, the fields were ploughed, seed sown and pine trees planted. This was done to prevent people from digging and searching the place. So Auschwitz, which was not destroyed by the Nazis due to lack of time – the Red Army was advancing faster than the Germans expected – is the only death camp preserved almost intact. This, combined with the fact that a museum devoted to the history of the camp has been created there, makes it easier for many people to associate Auschwitz with the *Endlösung*.

As Professor Ady Steg, the President of the *Alliance Israélite Universelle* wrote in *Regards* in 1987: 'Auschwitz is the symbol of the enterprise (unfortunately partially successful) to erase from the face of the earth a people, the Jewish people'. As such it concerns not only Jews, or the Jews, but the Jewish People.[12]

Two Views of a Common Past

The differences between the Polish and the Jewish memory of Auschwitz are symptomatic of the conflicting ways in which both communities approach their past. Despite the fact that the extermination of the Jews took place largely on Polish soil, the Holocaust was virtually ignored by the Poles for almost 40 years. The destruction of the Jews did not create a sense of collective shock amongst the Poles after the war. There were a variety of reasons for this, the main one being purely Polish losses and suffering. Between 1939 and 1945, approximately 10 per cent of the Polish Gentile population perished and the country lost altogether over six million of its citizens. The country was devastated, almost 40 per cent of the national wealth was destroyed, its industry and agriculture largely ruined. Some cities such as Warsaw were almost completely demolished. As a result there ensued a process which some authors (Irwin-Zarecka and others) have described as the 'Polonization of the Holocaust'.[13] Because the murdered Polish Jews have been consistently described in Polish historiography as Poles, people talk about the murder of six million Poles without distinguishing between their religious denominations. This was technically correct, since 2.9 million of the Polish Jews who perished were Polish citizens. However, it was wrong because it implied that both peoples had been equally treated by the Nazis. Indeed, both had endured brutal and inhuman treatment. However, only the Polish Jews had faced total extermination. Regardless of the large number of Polish Gentiles who died during the war, their fate cannot simply be equated with that of the Polish Jews. It was not correct to claim that they had suffered equally as nations and that they had suffered together. The Nazis forced the Jews to live in subhuman conditions which pushed them, for many Poles, beyond the pale of human solidarity. As Ewa Berberyusz suggested, in the case of the Jews a certain line was crossed which, instead of mobilizing support from the surrounding society, had the opposite effect – it paralysed and 'made it easier' to ignore them, isolating the Jews as never before.[14] The degradation imposed upon the Jews facilitated such an attitude and helped to drive a wedge between the two communities.

Another reason for the lack of reflection by Gentile Poles about the fate of the Jews was related to the behaviour of the Poles during the war. From the beginning until the end of the Second World War Poles were actively engaged in fighting the Nazis. About 350,000 people took part in various underground formations and a further 100,000 were soldiers of the Polish Armed Forces in the West. Polish participation in campaigns from France and the Battle of Britain through Narvik, Tobruk, and Monte Cassino to Arnhem and Berlin, made the Poles feel that they were a significant part of the war effort. By the end of the war, the Polish Forces constituted the fourth largest Allied army.

This constant support for the anti-Nazi effort created a feeling of self-righteousness among the Poles which made them reluctant to reflect on the less creditable aspects of their behaviour during the war. An additional cause for this was the fact that, in contrast to other occupied countries, there was no political collaboration between the Poles and the Germans. There were two main reasons for that. First, at the beginning of the war the Nazis did not look for political collaborators in Poland as they did in other countries. The Slavs in general were considered to be culturally and spiritually inferior (from mid-1941 the term *Untermensch* – the subhuman – was used) and thus unsuited for political alliances. The Poles in particular were much hated by the Nazis and were to be ruthlessly subjugated and their elite exterminated. In the later stages of the war the brutal policies of the Germans precluded any possibility of political collaboration. Secondly, those Poles who would in theory have been most inclined to cooperate with the Nazis – the proto-fascist and extreme right-wing parties which were traditionally strongly anti-semitic – were also historically extremely anti-German. This created a peculiar situation at the end of the war. Unlike right-wing groups in other East European countries who were compromised by their support for the Nazis, there was no crisis of right-wing ideology in Poland because even the extremist parties had fought against the Nazis (as well as against the Soviets) and could therefore be regarded as having been patriotic. As Aleksander Smolar pointed out in the West 'the traditional ethos of the right, compromised by spiritual kinship – however distant – with fascism, wartime collaboration, and anti-democratic tendencies, was clearly disintegrating. This was not the case in Poland, where the right was in equal parts patriotic, anti-German, anti-Soviet, and anti-semitic. Poland felt no need to rethink its values. There was no crisis of the rightist ethos'.[15]

This is not to suggest that there were no collaborators, denouncers, blackmailers, and traitors among the Gentile Poles, but the crucial difference to the European countries was that their support for the Nazis was not of a political or military nature. Despite the fact that the majority of Poles were profoundly anti-Soviet, the Nazis were never able to create a special unit like General Vlasov's Russian Liberation Army or the Ukrainian SS-Galizien. On the contrary, the appeal of right-wing anti-semitic ideology was strengthened by the sizeable Jewish presence in the ranks of the Communist Party and in the security apparatus in 1939–41 and in post-1945 Poland. Many small radical rightist parties contained in their xenophobic ideologies a stereotyped view of the Jew-Communist. This view, which was to some extent accepted by the less marginal political parties and by a considerable proportion of the Polish population, seemed to gain some credibility after the Soviet invasion of Poland and the ensuing Communist occupation of the Eastern borderlands between 17 September 1939 and 21 June 1941. As two Jewish historians, Pawel Korzec and Jean-Charles Szurek, admit, the Jewish youth and proletariat played an important ('although not exclusive') role in the apparatus of oppression, and implemented the 'class struggle' directed primarily against the Poles with 'revolutionary intransigence'.[16] At the same time, the Jewish community structure was destroyed, and eventually the non-communist political leaders and various socially active Jews were arrested and sent into the Soviet Union by the predominantly Jewish local militia. The Jewish response was not uniformally pro-communist and as a result many Jews were also deported. Soviet rule over this territory was very brutal. Out of 5 million Poles living in these territories, over 1.2 million were deported to the Soviet Union. This number included a quarter of a million children under 14 years of age. Almost half a million of the deportees were sent to prisons and labour camps where a large proportion of them perished.[17] The Jews, especially political, religious, and community leaders and activists, were not spared this treatment, but the overwhelming majority of those imprisoned and deported were Catholic Poles. Thus the Poles had a clear impression that they were fighting a war on two fronts while the Jews generally regarded the Soviets as a lesser evil than Hitler. As one Jewish witness explained:

16

The welcome extended to the Bolsheviks was above all a demon-stration of a separate identity, of being different from those against whom the Soviets were waging war – from the Poles – a refusal to be identified with the Polish state. We must not pre-tend that we do not realise this, or fail to admit that it was the result of our own policies and of our anti-semitism.[18]

The Jews were Polish citizens (even if they were sometimes treated as second class citizens) and the cooperation of some of them in the introduction of Stalinist terror to Eastern Poland was seen by others as contrary to the vital interests of the state and its citizens. As Aleksander Smolar observed:

> In no other European country during the war was there such a dramatic collision of interests and attitudes between the Jews and the nation among which they lived, as during the Soviet occupation 1939–41. Elsewhere Jews had discordant interests with a part of the society around them (for example with collaborators), but in solidarity, in a relationship with the rest of society. In eastern Poland, however, it was the Jews who were perceived as collaborators.[19]

Similarly, after the war the Party and the security apparatus were seen by a huge majority of Poles as acting against the basic interests of the nation. There was a tendency among the Poles to concentrate on the fact that these contained a disproportionately large number of Jewish Communists who, nevertheless, represented only a small percentage of the Jewish community as a whole. (This tendency glossed over the fact that the majority of Communist Party members and secret policemen were actually Polish Gentiles. This insistence, wholly without moral justification, of applying to another ethnic grouping standards of behaviour which they were unwilling to apply to themselves, enabled Poles to ignore their own participation in Stalinist crimes, and also encouraged the idea that no 'real Pole' could ever have committed such crimes against his or her own nation. Few Poles reflect on the fact that the creator of the largest and most bloody secret police organisation in history, the Cheka and its successors the NKVD, KGB and so on, was a Polish nobleman, Feliks Dzierżyński, as was his successor Henryk Yagoda. After all, thousands of Jews left Poland in 1945–47 because, other factors apart, they disliked and feared communism.) The Communist government itself encouraged this point of view which enabled it to label all anti-communists reactionary and anti-semitic, thus helping to discredit them in the eyes of many people in the West. A telling example of this policy was the fate of the Anti-Racist League, founded in 1946 by liberal-minded Gentiles of various political backgrounds, the purpose of which was to combat anti-semitism and influence public opinion. Since the establishment of the League was noted sympathetically in the American, British, and French press, the organisation was soon found unacceptable by the Communist government which forced it to concentrate on fighting against 'American and British imperialists persecuting negroes and other coloured peoples'. The Communists wanted to keep up the appearance of being the only 'progressive' group fighting anti-semitism. The Anti-Racist League, which refused to be side-tracked, was soon taken over and disbanded and many of its members found themselves in prison.[20]

Polish Responses to the Fate of the Jews

Under these circumstances no honest debate about the fate of the Jews was possible and most Poles failed to reflect on the difference between the Jewish-Polish and the Gentile-Polish experience. For the Jewish experience was very different indeed. It was easier to polonize Jewish suffering and to say that all Poles, Jews, and Gentiles had shared in it more or less equally. This attitude also helped to pacify the consciences of many people who might have felt that they had not done everything they could to help their Jewish neighbours. Because of the enforced segregation, isolation, and dehumanisation of the Jews by the Nazis, many Poles had, at the time, perceived them to be outside the community and a group to whom the common responsibilities of their society did not apply. Moreover, some Poles did not even believe that Jews belonged to Polish society and regarded them as aliens. Even those people who were ready to help the Jews during the war for humanitarian reasons could share this animosity towards them. The best-known example of such an attitude is Zofia Kossak-Szczucka, a co-founder of the Council for Aid to Jews (*Żegota*), a unique organisation in occupied Europe which provided help in the form of such things as shelter, money or false papers. In August 1942 she published an appeal which appeared as an underground leaflet calling the destruction of the Jews then in progress to be 'the most terrible crime history has ever witnessed', and stating that anyone who remained silent was an accomplice and that 'he who does not condemn, condones'. At the same time, the leaflet included a passage referring to the Jews as the political, economic, and ideological enemies of Poland. In the case of Kossak-Szczucka, this peculiar attitude was due to the old-fashioned and stereotypical view of the Jews which prevailed in many Catholic circles before the Second Vatican Council. It has to be said that she was generally very severe in her judgements of her own and other people's actions and of the mistakes she ascribed to them. In 1943–44, she was a prisoner in Auschwitz where she was subjected to and witnessed the suffering and humiliation of many women, including Polish Catholics like herself. In her diary published after the war under the title *From the Abyss*, she states quite clearly that the martyrdom of these Polish women was God's punishment for enjoying themselves before the war, for wearing lipstick or silk stockings. Her attitude to Jews, many of whom she helped personally, taking great risks, was characterized by the same old-fashioned outlook, typical of the *ancien régime*.[21]

Many Poles objected to what they perceived as the passivity of the Jews during the war. Poland is a country where resistance to the occupier had always been considered honourable. It was imperative to resist and those who did gained great respect and were ascribed heroic virtues. The Gentile Poles saw the exterminated Jewish masses as entirely passive. They thought that many more Jews could have saved themselves had they resisted. After all, even Emanuel Ringelblum – the famous Polish-Jewish historian murdered in March 1944 by the Nazis – was amazed by the apparent ease with which small groups of Nazi soldiers were able to control and put to death large numbers of Jews. In his diary he noted on 17 June 1942 that it was completely incomprehensible why Jews from various villages 'were evacuated under a guard of Jewish policemen. Not one of them escaped, although all of them knew where and towards what they were going ... One gendarme is sufficient to slaughter a whole town.' For many Gentile Poles this attitude, which confirmed stereotypes about the unsuitability of the Jews for any military activity and their cowardice (there were various popular derogatory sayings illustrating this such as 'as fit as a Jew with a rifle' or 'as brave as a Jew with a chained dog'), freed them from the necessity to reflect on the fate of the Jews and their own behaviour towards them. It also enabled them to disclaim any responsibility for what had happened to the Jews during the war and to preserve a clear conscience. As one nationalistic Pole put it quite recently, 'passive behaviour – seeking security by staying with the group and by accepting German orders – was the first and principle obstacle to the possibility of extending help to the Jews.'[22] Thus for the Poles the common perception of the past suggests that Gentile Poles fought bravely against the Nazis and against the Soviets while the Jews were indeed exterminated but by and large did nothing.

As Teresa Prekerowa pointed out, this is a highly stereotypical view of what constitutes resistance. The Poles are rightly proud not only of various forms of armed resistance organised during the war, but of civil resistance as well. The latter included the functioning of political parties underground, the existence of the underground press and education up to and including university level, as well as social and cultural activities. Indeed, this clandestine Poland is commonly referred to as the 'Underground State'. At the same time, as she says, the charge of Jewish passivity relates only to the lack of armed resistance. The Jews did nothing until they had nothing left to lose, when they started an uprising in the Warsaw ghetto on 19 April, 1943, and in Białystok shortly afterwards. Civil resistance also took place in some of the ghettos. There were political parties and youth organisations, underground newspapers and clandestine communications between the ghettos themselves and with the outside world. Some education was also provided clandestinely, in so-called *complets* for small groups of pupils meeting in private appartments, and some scientific research was even carried out (mainly medical investigation about the effects of hunger on people, published shortly after the war in Poland) and historical archives created.[23] The most famous such archive, entitled *Oneg Shabbat* and established in the Warsaw ghetto by Emanuel Ringelblum, is now one of the major sources of information about Jewish life in the ghetto.

The Polish stereotype ignores the fact that life in the ghetto was closer to that in any labour camp than to life on the Aryan side, in cities, so that it was incomparably more difficult to organize any form of resistance. Few Poles remember the Jewish presence in the Polish underground and among the Soviet partisans, or about the armed revolts that broke out in some extermination camps.

The romanticized self-image of the Poles has also been relevant to the fate of Poland after the Second World War. Since the majority of Poles believed that they were gallant allies, whose efforts contributed substantially towards the war effort, the result of the Teheran and Yalta conferences, when it eventually became public knowledge, came as a devastating shock to the nation. The Poles perceived themselves as one of the main victims of the war and hoped to get some compensation after the Nazis had been defeated. Instead, in 1945, Poles were left with a country which had been through five years of suffering and destruction and which now, despite their active resistance and the loss of six million citizens, found itself deprived of half her historic territories and, worse still, subjugated once more by a foreign power. There was a universally felt sense of outrage and dismay at the Western Allies who failed Poland twice – in 1939 by declaring war but failing to act on their declaration, and in 1945 by transferring the country into the Soviet sphere of interest. In the first half of the 19th century Poles had accepted an old Russian Panslavic idea that the suffering of the Slavs served as a penance for the whole of Christendom. In the aftermath of the failed uprising against the Russians in 1830–31 the Poles developed a tendency to regard themselves as the martyrs of history, 'the Christ of nations'. But, although the Romantic poet Adam Mickiewicz who propagated this messianic notion considered the Jews to be the 'older brother' of the Polish nation sharing in this martyrdom, the majority of Poles after the Second World War were not inclined to reflect on the suffering of others. As Ezra Mendelsohn once remarked in this context, it is often difficult for a victim to see that someone else may also be one.

Shoah: *Jewish Reactions to Polish Conduct During the War*

The Jews, on the other hand, regard themselves as the principal victim of the war and have a tendency to downplay or ignore the fate of the Polish Gentiles. The most influential exponent of the Jewish approach to the Holocaust has been Claude Lanzmann, the creator and director of the monumental film *Shoah* (the Hebrew word meaning 'destruction', and as such much more appropriate than 'holocaust', which means 'burnt offering'). This nine-and-a-half-hour film, based entirely on contemporary footage, consists largely of interviews with the Jewish survivors of the death and concentration camps, the Polish witnesses to the destruction, and even some of the German perpetrators. The film's austere and matter-of-fact format made a strong impact on viewers throughout the world. Although devoted entirely to the history of the extermination of the Jews, it is neither a documentary nor a feature film. It remains in a class of its own. It is a strong personal statement and an attempt to re-create the past. Powerful and important as the film is, it contains some serious flaws as well. Its impact was such that one could analyse it effectively only after reflection. *Shoah* was a cinematographic masterpiece of great moral significance, but it was also intended to (and did) become a source of historical knowledge for a wider public.

One of the major problems facing the critic of an historical film is what criteria to apply to judging it. Is it a documentary or is it a work of fiction? If it is an historical fiction, to what extent is it based on historical truth? Lanzmann himself stressed emphatically that *Shoah* was not a documentary; it was a work of art (although it is not obvious that these two are mutually exclusive). Lanzmann claimed, however, that his was a work of art which was historically accurate in every respect and detail and that nothing essential, particularly about Polish history, had been omitted. During an international conference organised by the Institute for Polish-Jewish Studies in Oxford in 1985 at which *Shoah* had its British premiere, Lanzmann boldly claimed that he was the leading specialist on the Holocaust and was therefore very reluctant to accept the slightest criticism from professional historians. Lanzmann's claim that everything in the film was absolutely accurate made his position untenable. Since *Shoah* consists entirely of interviews, without any narrative coming from the director (the American publishers of the screen-play of the film advertised it as 'an oral history of the Holocaust'), what could Lanzmann's claim mean? Only one thing – that when Lanzmann heard historically inaccurate statements, he corrected them during his filmed conversations or edited them afterwards. (Out of 350 hours of filmed material *Shoah* used nine and a half, providing ample scope for editing.) This, however, was not the case. It is not at all surprising that in a work of this magnitude there should be some factual mistakes. Anyone who specialises in oral history or anthropology knows that people talking about the past make numerous mistakes about dates, places, names, and other facts. This may not be of crucial importance, but it is necessary to acknowledge the phenomenon and a special methodology is required to deal with it. No one expects total accuracy in accounts of events which took place 45–50 years ago given by witnesses. In *Shoah* there are a number of small mistakes, something not very important in itself, but interesting because Lanzmann denies it vehemently. There are also more important ones, some related to the history of Auschwitz-Birkenau.

For example, in the testimony of a survivor, Rudolf Vrba (registered in the camp as Walter Rosenberg, no 44070), who was in Auschwitz from 30 June 1942 until his escape on 7 April 1944, he stated that he was the first prisoner to escape, bringing information to the outside world about life in the camp, including the mass extermination of Jews. Vrba said in the film that the underground movement in the camp 'was organised by German-speaking people, whose aim was to improve living conditions in the camp and to survive. They were to a certain extent successful, fewer people were dying, and as the camp was always overcrowded, the only result of this movement was that more Jews were sent to the gas chambers.' This prompted a strong rebuttal from a Polish historian of Auschwitz and an ex-inmate, Jozef Garliński, who pointed out to Lanzmann that Vrba expressed different views both in a private letter addressed to himself and in his book *Factory of Death* published 20 years earlier.[24] This criticism was rejected by Lanzmann in an unpleasant manner. Nevertheless it remains true that the film gave a false impression about that part of Auschwitz which was a concentration camp. The first escape from the camp actually occurred on 6 July 1940 and many others followed before that of Vrba (altogether 667 prisoners tried to escape and 397 were successful). Vrba was not the first person to bring news about the extermination of the Jews to the outside world, although he was one of the two people who reported on the preparations in the camp for the liquidation of Jews from Hungary. The underground in Auschwitz was already organised in October 1940 by an officer in the underground Polish Army – Witold Pilecki – who had himself sent to Auschwitz for that very purpose. Throughout the life of the camp the underground there was controlled by the Poles who used German as a *lingua franca* to communicate with prisoners of other nationalities. The main role of the underground was to prepare for the final fight for the camp with the help of the Home Army units and the advancing Soviet Army. However, there was no contact with the Red Army and the Home Army agreed to assist the prisoners only if the Nazis started to liquidate the camp together with all prisoners, which in the end did not happen. The camp's underground organised escapes and sent couriers to the commander of the Home Army and tried to help the prisoners. Its activities had no bearing whatsoever on the fate of the Jews in the negative way suggested by Vrba.

The greatest of Lanzmann's sins are those of omission. These are linked to the history of Polish-Jewish relations during the war. *Shoah* is a film *à thèse* and shows only those things which support the director's thesis. The Polish backdrop of the film which plays a large role in it is set out in a way which fits Lanzmann's preconceptions. Those aspects of conditions in occupied Poland which could contradict the *thèse* are consistently and conspicuously ignored. When Lanzmann said in Oxford that 'nothing essential' about the Poles was left out, it is not too strong to claim that he was falsifying history. The historians present and the journalist, Ash, who wrote the first major review of the film (published in *The New York Review of Books*) admitted as much. The film contains no material which does not support Lanzmann's point of view. Since it is constructed around people and their recollections, the key problem is that of selection. Who is to be shown and interviewed, and who may be left out? What are the criteria for selection? Is the final result fair, representative, and complete? Characteristically Lanzmann refused to answer this question in Oxford. After a long and heated exchange with academics, he eventually admitted that these criteria were his 'obsessions'. This is of course perfectly acceptable if the work does not pretend to be history. In this respect however the film does not so much re-create history as create it. This may seem a harsh judgement, especially as the film is very moving, but it is inevitable if the film is to be judged by the rules applicable to the examination of historical works.

Lanzmann decided not to interview or show people who would tell stories that he did not like, irrespective of their importance. These included the head of the first separate Jewish Section of the Bureau of Information and Propaganda of the Chief Command of the Home Army, Henryk Woliński, and Marek Edelman, one of the commanders of the Jewish Fighting Organisation (ŻOB) during the Warsaw ghetto uprising. In Oxford he gave numerous explanations for various noticeable omissions. Some people were 'weak' on the screen, could not 're-live the past'; others wanted to lecture him, some were busy or ill. All these excuses are legitimate for an artist, but not for an historian. Worse still, the people who were not included fell into certain categories, which, as a result were not represented. It appeared that not a single Pole helped Jews during the war, and yet those who survived had to rely almost exclusively on Polish help. Members of the Jewish Resistance were virtually ignored as well. It is clear that Lanzmann's *thèse* would have been seriously weakened by the evidence provided by these witnesses. The idea that Jews went to their death because the Poles were totally indifferent could not have been sustained. It is not that the Poles should not, or could not have done more to help the Jews, but historically the terrible truth remains that the overwhelming majority of Polish Jews were doomed, regardless of the degree of Polish help or Jewish resistance. Both could have been safely mentioned in *Shoah* without fear that the central message would somehow have become blurred. The problem is that by ignoring them, Lanzmann forfeited his claim to present historical truth accurately. The excuses he offered in Oxford were intellectually dishonest. There is also the troubling factor of the manipulation of the material. This has been pointed out by one of Lanzmann's interviewees, Jan Karski. Karski was the courier for the Polish underground who in 1942 succeeded in bringing to the West information about the extermination of Jews and the appeals for help. He was the first person to talk to Anthony Eden, Roosevelt and others about the desperate position of Polish Jews – all in vain. And yet Lanzmann, out of eight hours of interview with Karski, decided to show his description of the suffering in the ghetto and to ignore the only part of the testimony which makes it absolutely unique. Karski himself has commented on this:

> The inclusion of this material in the film, as well as even general information about those who tried to help Jews, would have presented the destruction of Jews in a proper historical perspective. Leaders of nations, powerful governments decided about this destruction or participated in this destruction, or kept indifferent towards it. People, normal people, thousands of people sympathised with the Jews or helped them.[25]

The whole issue of the film parallels that of the Carmelite convent. Both emerged roughly at the same time, both are related to the central problem of contradictory perceptions of the common past existing in the Polish and Jewish communities. The manipulation of history on both sides can be seen in *Shoah* and in many Polish writings on the Holocaust in general, and Auschwitz in particular.

The film provoked a furious debate in Poland and abroad. The Polish government went so far as to issue a *démarche* to the French government in which they requested that the film should not be screened in France as it contained slanderous anti-Polish propaganda. Most critical articles appeared in Poland before any Pole had actually seen the film. The government later changed its attitude and allowed *Shoah* to be screened on Polish television and in cinemas. This was followed by more discussions in the media which were on the whole less critical than before. The authorities, cautious not to appear anti-semitic in the West, permitted a degree of free discussion at least in the spheres of Jewish culture and history. At the same time, they clearly intimated that the presentation of various issues in Polish-Jewish history and Polish-Jewish relations affect the country's image abroad. Jaruzelski's government behaved throughout in an incoherent manner, sometimes accusing the Church (especially in its attitudes before the War) of anti-semitism and on other occasions defending the Church in order to attack certain liberal intellectuals. *Shoah* was a case in point. At first attacked on the grounds that it was anti-Polish, it was later defended by pro-Communist journalists on the grounds that Lanzmann did not criticize the Poles but rather the Church. Thus Zygmunt Kałużyński, a film critic writing for the Party weekly *Polityka* (edited at the time by Mieczysław Rakowski who was soon to become first secretary of the Communist Party), attacked the Church, blaming it for anti-semitism. According to Kałużyński, people who attacked Lanzmann in Poland were attempting not only to forget the shameful record of Christians, but also to absolve the Church from all responsibility by showing Polish anti-semitism as a social, psychological, economic, and political phenomenon, rather than a religious one.[26] At the same time, Jerzy Turowicz, one of the people attacked by Kałużyński, wrote a critique of the film in which he criticized the anti-semitism of Polish Catholics, stating openly that anti-semitism cannot be reconciled with Christianity. He also admitted that the Polish Catholics 'who were the witnesses of the tragic fate of the Jewish nation on (Polish soil) seeing what anti-semitism could lead to, should have conducted a deep soul searching as far as the sin of anti-semitism was concerned ... such settling of accounts – in my judgement has not been done yet.'[27]

At the same time, Turowicz criticized *Shoah* for not being objective but rather tendentious in its portrayal of Poles, reflecting instead simplified and stereotypical views prevalent in the West and ultimately anti-Polish. Poles in the West, especially those in the United States, organised numerous protest actions and attempted to boycott the film, demonstrating an oversensitivity which suggested that they were not yet ready for a calm evaluation of the problem. The self-image of the Poles has not changed substantially since the War as far as the Polish-Jewish issue is concerned. Few people were ready to question it, although *Shoah*, the Błoński controversy (see Ch. 5), and the conflict over the Carmelite convent have seriously challenged it. Conversely, the popular Jewish view of the Holocaust and of the behaviour of the Poles and the Church was strengthened by *Shoah* as it was by the establishment of the Carmel.

Poles – 'The Worst Anti-Semites'

The view presented by Claude Lanzmann's *Shoah* is widely shared by sizeable portions of the Jewish community. Lanzmann's general theory is first, that the Holocaust was the logical conclusion of centuries of anti-semitism (verbalized in the film by Raoul Hilberg), and secondly that the Jews were abandoned to their fate while bystanders to their tragedy (mainly Poles, as the destruction of European Jewry took place among them) looked on passively. 'They mastered the routine of extermination. No one was troubled by it.'[28] For Lanzmann, as for many others, the war-time world was divided into three groups: the victims (the Jews), the murderers (the Nazis and their collaborators), and the bystanders, who were by and large not only passive but also unsympathetic. Thus the Gentiles in general and Poles in particular are seen as partially responsible for, or even guilty of, the extermination of the Jews. Poles are considered to be traditional anti-semites of an especially virulent kind who as such found it natural to sympathise with Hitler's anti-semitic policies, even though they opposed him on other grounds. Even some serious Jewish scholars regarded large sections of Polish society as playing a major role in exacerbating the plight of the Jews: 'influenced by the Nazis anti-Jewish policy, they not only supported the Nazi programme being executed in Poland but actually bettered it by exposing Jews in hiding or those who tried to change their identity. Many of the Jews who escaped and took shelter among the Poles were first blackmailed and then handed over to the Germans by the gangs of *szmalcownicy* or extortionists.'[29] The argument that Auschwitz was located in Poland because Hitler was certain of Polish cooperation in his extermination of the Jews is commonplace, as is the view expressed by Lanzmann that what happened in Poland could not have happened, for instance, in France, where extermination camps would have been impossible. This is an arrogant and morally dubious statement not confirmed by historical research on France during the war. As Marrus and Paxton showed (*Vichy France and the Jews*, 1981), French help to the SS was indispensable in identifying, enumerating, and isolating Jews in internment camps and handing them over to the Nazis entirely on their own initiative. Vichy offered more substantial help to the Nazis than any other Western European country and most East European countries including even German allies such as Rumania and Hungary.

Unlike the Danes or the Dutch, Poles were considered by many Jews to be unwilling to help and worse, sympathetic to Hitler's actions. This comparison shows a lack of understanding of the conditions existing in those countries under Nazi occupation. The penalties in Poland for helping Jews were the most draconian in occupied Europe. Any kind of aid was automatically punishable by the death of entire families. The Dutch also had their share of blackmailers and collaborators. Anne Frank was denounced by a Dutchman and the Dutch SS fought alongside their German equivalent. The percentage of Jews saved in the Netherlands is about the same as that saved in Poland, yet the Dutch are not considered either particularly anti-semitic, or to have a bad war-record – in fact the opposite. In Denmark, King Christian X and his subjects were very friendly to the local Jewish community which was, however, minute – comprising about 7,800 people, including 1,300 half-Jews. In a remarkable display of solidarity, in October 1943, 90 per cent of them were transported to Sweden and thus saved.[30] This action notwithstanding, it is impossible directly to compare the terror which existed in Poland from 1939 onwards with the occupation of Denmark. The scale of the problem, due to the different size of the Jewish communities in the two countries, makes the comparison invalid. In 1939 there were around 3.5 million Jews in Poland. Even in Denmark, there were some pro-Nazi Danes who betrayed the Jews, of whom a few hundred ended up in a concentration camp in Theresienstadt. Thus while the Poles should not be excused – much more could have been done – they should not be singled out either. The huge majority of Polish Jews would have been murdered irrespective of anything that the Poles could have done. The question at issue therefore is rather the morality of Polish attitudes towards the destruction of the Jewish community – their apparent indifference – rather than the historical facts, on which most historians by now agree.

Many in the Jewish community consider the Holocaust to be a purely Jewish phenomenon, and are unaware of the fact that Polish Gentiles were also killed on the theory that any intelligent Pole might be a potential threat to the new German order. While the Polish masses are criticised or condemned for their reluctance to help the Jews, and those unscrupulous individuals who benefitted materially and in other ways from the Jewish tragedy are rightly viewed with contempt, a double standard is applied towards those members of the Jewish community who worked in Jewish councils, the *Judenrate*. These were a form of Jewish municipal self-government introduced by the Germans. With little real power or scope for action, their main function was to alleviate the conditions of the ghetto population and (in direct contradiction) to carry out German orders facilitating the destruction of this population. The members of the *Judenrate*, (mainly Jewish collaborators, but also including people of good will who hoped to be able to help the others), are excused, on the grounds that they had little choice, much more willingly than those Gentiles whose caution and fear prevented them from offering help to the Jews, or even actively opposing the Nazis.

Most Poles particularly resent the application of this double standard to those Jewish individuals who were active in, and high-ranking members of, the Communist Party, and especially of the security police. These are sometimes excused on the grounds that Communist ideology offered them hope of achieving equal status with the Gentile population and of living in a country free of anti-semitism where social justice and liberal ideals would prevail. It is also often suggested that the Jews, being more vulnerable because of their ethnic background, had no choice but to participate in the construction of the new order. This view is offensive both to the majority of the Jews who did not want to live under Communism and left Poland, and because it implies that different moral standards can be applied to judge Jewish and Gentile moral behaviour. It is important to make a distinction here between those who supported and joined the Communist Party and even became its propagandists and activists for whatever misguided reason, and those who were directly involved in the security apparatus. The latter involved active participation in arrests and interrogations, and thus torture, deportations, and, in some instances, killing of the civilian population. One can treat the former cases with some sympathy and understanding, but it is not possible to excuse the latter. Whatever the conditions existing in Poland between 1945 and 1956, no one – Gentile or Jewish – can claim that he or (very often) she *had* to be a member of the Stalinist political police or the judiciary and, for one reason or another, had no choice but to torture and kill their innocent political opponents. After all, no one looks for extenuating circumstances for ex-members of the Gestapo.

The Poles have not been much given to introspection about the darker areas of their past. This was limited, by and large, to a small group of intellectuals, a fact which has been rightly criticized by many Jews. At the same time, the Jewish community, which is generally more inclined towards self-examination, tends to be uncritical of the behaviour of some members of its own community. When describing the extensive (although never precisely established) Jewish cooperation with Soviet officials and the NKVD in Eastern Poland between 1939 and 1941, the historians Korzec and Szurek object to the use of terms such as 'betrayal' and 'collaboration' which many Poles would consider appropriate. The same applies to the Jewish communists who enforced the Soviet system in Poland after 1944. While rejecting any blanket condemnation based on racial stereotypes, it is nevertheless possible to examine these phenomena from a slightly more critical standpoint. As Simon Wiesenthal said in an interview given on his 80th birthday:

> Then the war came. It is at times like these that the lower elements in society surface – the *szmalcownicy* (blackmailers) who would betray Jews for a bottle of vodka or a pair of shoes. That was one aspect. On the other hand the 30 or 40,000 Jews who survived, survived thanks to help from Poles. This I know. But on the other hand whenever I am talking on this subject I always say that I know what kind of role Jewish communists played in Poland after the war. And just as I, as a Jew, do not want to shoulder responsibility for the Jewish communists, I cannot blame 36 million Poles for those thousands of *szmalcownicy*.[31]

CHAPTER 3

The Conflict Begins

The Conflict Comes to Poland

The conflict about the camp was brought to Poland in December 1985 when the President of the World Jewish Congress, Edgar Bronfman, visited Poland and discussed the issue with the then Minister for Religious Affairs, Adam Łopatka. The Minister agreed that the Government would try to negotiate with the Church to move the convent. The Church itself was not approached directly and the government claimed later that they could not reverse the Church's decision. The first contact with the Church took place in February 1986 when a small delegation of Belgian Jewish leaders, consisting of Markus Pardes, President of the Coordinating Committee of Jewish Organisations in Belgium, Albert Guigui, Rabbi to the *Consistoire Central Israélite de Belgique*, Nathan Ramet, an ex-prisoner of Auschwitz, and David Susskind, President of the *Centre Communautaire Laic Juif*, visited Poland. Their initial exchanges with Cardinal Macharski have already been discussed in the introduction. The general feeling was that the visit was just the opening of the dialogue on this matter which was welcomed by Cardinal Macharski who regretted that no such meeting had taken place before and hoped that a solution satisfactory to all sides could be found.

The Jewish position was elaborated at a meeting with Minister Łopatka. The Jewish delegation was surprised that a decision concerning the convent could have been taken without consultating the Jewish community. The government's position was that it had total authority to take decisions related to the territory over which it had sovereignty and that such decisions did not have to be taken in consultation with any foreigners. The Belgian delegation disagreed, claiming that everything related to Auschwitz had an international dimension.[1]

In March 1986, Cardinal Franciszek Macharski explained the reasons for placing a Catholic convent in Auschwitz in an article published by *Tygodnik Powszechny*, a liberal Catholic weekly. This weekly, which has appeared continuously for 45 years with the exception of a period between March 1953 and the end of 1956 when it was closed down for its refusal to publish an obituary of Stalin, has a very large following in Poland, especially among the intelligentsia. Until recently, it was the most independent newspaper published officially in Poland, though heavily censored and artificially restricted in its circulation by the authorities. Its official circulation figure of 80,000 has never reflected its real readership which is closer to 250,000 people. A very high quality newspaper, it has considerable influence and is an important moulder of opinion. Over the years, *Tygodnik Powszechny* has published many articles on Polish-Jewish relations and their history. Its editor since 1945, Jerzy Turowicz, has always taken a keen interest in Polish-Jewish dialogue. The critics of *Tygodnik*, most of whom come from communist circles, have often described the paper as philosemitic. In his article, Cardinal Macharski presented the Carmelite convent as a Christian way to tackle the spiritual challenge of the camp. The main issue for him was that the tragedy of Auschwitz should be remembered: 'The record of it should constantly be renewed, also in the religious dimension of man's awareness and conscience. It must be renewed both on account of the passage of time and because of the deliberate attempts to obliterate and distort that crime. Without remembering there would be no admonition and warning.' For the Cardinal, Auschwitz-Birkenau was a 'new sacred place which belongs at the same time to all humanity and to every nation', although he also stressed, quoting the Pope's visit there in 1979, that it was a place of terrifying tragedy for the Jewish people and pointed out that it was in the camps of Majdanek and Birkenau that 'the best-known symbols of this extermination' are to be seen. He expanded on the uniqueness of the destruction which faced the Jewish nation by saying that the tragedy was 'particularly frightful not only because of its magnitude in terms of the number of victims but also because that nation had been condemned by Hitlerite racism to total and immediate annihilation.' At the same time, Macharski distinguished between the meaning of Birkenau and that of Auschwitz to which, according to him, the Poles also have a claim: 'German racism destined the Slavs for slavery and cultural as well as biological degradation which was actually started during the war. For the Poles Oświęcim is a synonym of martyrdom and extermination which affected the majority of families.' The two Christian martyrs, St Maximilian

Kolbe and Edith Stein, who perished in the camp upholding their Christian faith, represent the Church's attitude towards the Nazi crimes. By venerating these two, the Church pays homage to all the other victims. The fact that Edith Stein became Sister Benedicta of the Cross after her conversion, and a member of the Carmelite Order, made it particularly appropriate for the Polish Discalced Carmelite nuns[2] 'to express their communion with their sister' Edith Stein in the place where she was murdered. The convent devoted to her and to Fr Kolbe's memory would, according to Macharski, honour all the other victims of the camp: 'The Catholic Church also holds in great reverence the sacrifice of four million people – men, women and children – of different faiths and ideologies. We are sure there were many 'nameless' heroes among them, who by their humanity were gaining victories over a system of denial of the dignity and the rights of man. Of the victims known to us by name the Church mentions two figures – and through them pays homage to each and every victim.'

Explaining the nature of the Discalced Carmelite Order, Macharski stated that according to their rule, the nuns lived within the confines of the convent and devoted themselves to prayer and penance, which in this case was to serve as expiation for the crimes committed in Auschwitz-Birkenau and for peace and unity in the world. Their very presence served to confirm that charity was possible and stronger than evil. Macharski also showed his appreciation of the spiritual dimension of the nuns' decision. They had 'in a way condemned themselves to perpetual endurance in the proximity of the site of a terrifying crime of genocide.' In this context, the Cardinal mentioned that a precedent for establishing a convent in Auschwitz was another Carmelite convent already established at Dachau concentration camp in Germany. Lastly, Macharski pointed out that the convent was situated outside the camp's boundaries. The building, which is located outside the fence, was chosen because of its close proximity to Block XI which contained the 'hunger bunker', the place of death for many victims, including St Maximilian Kolbe.[3]

Faced with criticism from Jewish circles, Cardinal Macharski outlined his position in a letter addressed to Dr Victor Goldbloom, President of the International Council of Christians and Jews in April 1986, including as one more reason for the convent's presence the argument that many Nazis had been nominally Christian:

It was not a spirit of triumphalism or proselytism, not an attempt to erase the memory of the losses inflicted on the Jews at that place: finally, it was not a desire to appropriate the symbolism of the place by the Christians. We wanted only to set a sign reminding what that place was in reality, a sign indicating what lesson should be taken from it: not a material sign which would become one more exposition but a living spiritual sign ... the living monument of expiation for crimes done by men of the past, among whom there were also those who had been Christians before they clung to the Nazi ideology.[4]

Diverging Theologies

The two elements of Macharski's statements – the distinction made between Auschwitz and Birkenau and the location of the convent outside the boundaries of Auschwitz – were soon to become hotly contested issues. The theological language used by Macharski referring to Christian charity, expiation of sins, penance, martyrdom and so on, created further problems with a Jewish community unaccustomed to and often offended by such terminology. In March of that year, representatives of various European and American Jewish organisations set up a committee based in Paris to coordinate the campaign against the convent. The same month, the International Council of the Anti-Defamation League, B'nai B'rith, issued a statement stressing the international status of Auschwitz and discussing the issue of legal responsibility for the camp. The question of the convent's location in relation to the camp was also raised. The B'nai B'rith document attempted to establish that there was some international jurisdiction over Auschwitz-Birkenau. According to B'nai B'rith, in 1972 UNESCO adopted a Convention for the Protection of the World Cultural and National Heritage which was ratified by Poland four years later. In 1978, the Polish government requested that the camp be added to the World Heritage List which includes cultural and natural sites of outstanding importance. The application included a map of the area and a list of the buildings which were to be protected. Both contained the old theatre despite the fact that it was located outside the perimeter. The Polish application was accepted in 1979.[5] Thus, B'nai B'rith argued, the building where the convent was located was definitely part of the site and therefore the convention allowed for a degree of foreign control over it.

Different theological interpretations about the nature of the site of the camp were voiced by various Jewish leaders. In April 1986, a group of leading European rabbis sent a letter to the Pope expressing their disquiet over the convent. While Cardinal Macharski spoke about a new holy place, the rabbis found it 'utterly incongruent to sanctify ground which is desecrated and accursed, drenched with the blood of victims brutally tormented and slaughtered in history's greatest genocide. The very world Auschwitz has become synonymous with the Holocaust, and to have this place of infinite inhumanity serve as a religious shrine would cause affront and agony, particularly to the survivors of that infamous camp and their families.' The rabbis reminded the Pope that there had been a proposal to erect a Jewish monument in Auschwitz, a project which was 'turned down on the grounds that there shouldn't be a reference to any particular religious faith' although most victims of the camp were Jewish and murdered for that sole reason. Therefore, the rabbis asserted, constructing a place of worship for another faith was even more objectionable, especially since the majority of the Nazis were nominally Christian.[6]

The following month the European Jewish Congress passed a resolution which confirmed that the Jews considered the Carmelite presence in Auschwitz to be an affront to all Jews. The Congress urged the Church and the Polish government to remove the convent in order not to jeopardise Catholic-Jewish dialogue.

> 'Without questioning the sincerity and piety of the Carmelite nuns, we reaffirm the conviction that the memory of the millions of Jews and Gentiles murdered by Nazi fascism can best be preserved and honoured by maintaining the site where history's most horrendous slaughter was perpetrated as a silent reminder of man's capacity for evil, without the symbols of any particular religion and equivocal acts of forgiveness.'

Here again, Catholic categories of repentance, expiation, and forgiveness were totally at odds with Jewish theology. Carmelite prayer at Auschwitz was seen by the Jewish community as deeply offensive, especially in view of the Church's behaviour during the war:

> When our brothers and sisters met their death in Auschwitz, they were surrounded by a total silence on the part of the world and a very significant silence on the part of the Church. We cannot tolerate that prayers should take place, even in the best

of intentions, in this place, from those who could have, at the right time, raised their voice for our brothers and sisters and who did not do so.[7]

Thus, as Markus Pardes insisted, the only way to honour the dead was to maintain the site 'in total silence, the silence that was the silence of man and the silence of God'.

Clearly, some Jewish leaders had a very uneasy relationship with the Catholic Church despite the changes which had taken place since the Second Vatican Council. The historical disagreements, especially concerning the role of the Vatican and Pope Pius XII during the war and the anti-semitism of the Polish people and clergy in particular, formed a constant background to any discussions, even though they were not openly raised.

Western Catholics Criticize the Poles

The Polish aspect of the debate in particular was little understood even by many Western Catholics. Many Catholic and Protestant organisations interested in dialogue with Judaism shared the Jewish position on the issue. The problem was the differing historical and symbolic interpretation of the camp. Few Western Catholics had any notion of what Auschwitz meant for the Gentile Poles or had any understanding of other aspects of the impact of the Second World War on the Polish people. Thus the news about the convent was widely misunderstood. In the collective imagination of most Western Christians other than the Poles, Auschwitz is a Jewish camp and the symbol of the *Shoah*. Monsignor Matagrin, President of the French Episcopal Committee for Relations with Judaism, stated that the siting of the Carmel in Auschwitz could not be accepted because the tragedy of the *Shoah* gave the Jewish people an inalienable moral right to Auschwitz.[8] Others stated that the Carmelite presence was unacceptable despite the good intentions which had inspired the nuns. Fr Bernard Dupuy, secretary of the French Episcopal Committee for Relations with Judaism, even implied that the nuns could have been motivated by considerations other than the desire to repent.[9] Over 1100 Belgian Christians published a petition expressing their distress at this turn of events, showing much more sensitivity than their Polish equivalents. Recognizing the symbolic importance of Auschwitz for the Jews, they also recognized its emotional significance in Jewish sensibility. They were saddened and distressed by the fact that a Christian project could offend the Jews whom they referred to as brothers and applauded the willingness of the Carmelites to contribute actively to reconciliation between Christians and Jews. At the same time, they noted that the convent in Auschwitz did not serve this intention and, in fact, made such a reconciliation more difficult. For that reason alone, they urged the Polish Church and the Polish authorities to arrange the transfer of the convent and by doing so to remove the source of conflict between the communities. Many French and Belgian Catholics (for a long time interest in the affair was limited to the French-speaking community) regarded the affair as blown up out of all proportion by the press and some shared the point of view of the Polish Catholic Church.

The Primate Intervenes

The Primate of Poland, Cardinal Józef Glemp, was confronted with the problem for the first time in April 1986 during his trip to France where he met a delegation of French Jewish representatives and promised to convey their objections to the relevant Church authorities in Poland. At a press conference in Paris, he elaborated on his response to the Jewish community. He stated that he did not understand what lay at the bottom of the problem and requested a written presentation of 'rational arguments'. He said it was necessary to recompense God for this horrific sin by praying at the site of this extermination camp where the blood of innocent Russians, Poles, Dutchmen, Jews, and Austrians had flowed. He then complained about the violent attacks from all sides directed against the Polish Church which he did not like at all because, he said, 'people do not give us rational reasons' and because 'they do not talk to the Episcopate'. 'After all, we have Jews in Poland, we have rabbis, and no one has protested or objected to the Polish Episcopate.' He hoped that the whole matter would be calmly resolved between both parties because it was the Polish and Jewish nations who had suffered most during the Second World War. These two peoples had a parallel destiny and it was not possible to create an antagonism between them. Moreover, Cardinal Glemp rejected the accusation of Polish anti-semitism which he considered to be a myth created by the enemies of the country.[10]

This first intervention by the Polish Primate in the controversy was a portent of things to come. The Primate not only failed to show much sensitivity, but he was also undiplomatic and badly informed. His repeated requests for 'rational arguments' were largely a result of his legal background. He has a doctorate in Civil and Canon Law from the Lateran University in Rome and tends to look at issues from a narrow legal perspective which can be particularly inappropriate where moral and symbolic issues are concerned. As Primate and President of the Episcopate, he takes his authority very seriously, aware of the hundreds of years of tradition behind this position, particularly in Poland. This explains his insistence on procedure and matters being resolved via appropriate channels. At the same time, his presentation of history was somewhat maladroit. The Auschwitz-Birkenau complex was divided into two main parts – the concentration and the extermination camps. The inmates of the former represented over 30 different nationalities, but the majority were always Polish. The victims of the extermination camp, which Cardinal Glemp referred to, were 90 per cent Jewish. Although they came from a variety of countries, they were murdered there specifically as Jews. Cardinal Glemp, who talked about the 6,230,000 Polish victims of the Second World War, failed to make a clear distinction between the origin and fate of the victims. His exposé showed a tendency to Polonize the Holocaust, undermining the greater understanding shown by Cardinal Macharski of the difference between Auschwitz and Birkenau.

Polish Jews: A Muted First Response

The Cardinal also raised an interesting point about the relative lack of reaction on the part of the Jewish community in Poland, which is admittedly very small – consisting of not more than a few thousand people. The Jews living in Poland were not particularly incensed by the creation of the Carmel in Auschwitz. A variety of views were expressed. These ranged from the conviction that one should not build any religious monument on the tombs of millions of Jews, Poles, Russians, and others, rather honouring the memory of the victims by maintaining silence, to the view that the convent, although inappropriately located, was less objectionable than the museum in the camp, which was felt to contain historically inaccurate information and created the impression that the camp was some kind of tourist attraction. In general, Polish Jews felt that the creation of the convent was not the result of bad faith on the part of the Church, or evil intentions, but rather ignorance about Jewish matters, and lack of sensitivity. On the other hand, a well-known Polish Jewish intellectual of the younger generation and frequent spokesman on Jewish issues (a member of the Polish Government's Commission on the Future of Auschwitz), Dr Stanisław Krajewski, published an article in *Tygodnik Powszechny* which defended the sisters.[11] Krajewski pointed out that the whole controversy was fraught with misunderstandings from the outset. The text of the original appeal published in Belgium contained phrases about the 'conversion of strayed brothers', and a reference to Edith Stein's attainment of eternal life and seemed to imply that Jewish victims who, unlike Edith Stein, were not baptised, would not achieve eternal life. This was interpreted by Jewish circles in the West as the beginning of a Catholic proselyting offensive. Krajewski rejected this conclusion and the accusations of triumphalism on the part of the Church on the grounds that they came from Western Jews who often displayed prejudice 'which occasionally developed into hatred towards the Church, Poland, and, in particular towards the Polish Church, as guilty of dark deeds'. Krajewski explained that in reality, prayer was the sisters' only aim. He considered the presence of a contemplative community most appropriate in these awesome surroundings, and he thought that to pray was the best thing a person could do there. Moreover he pointed out that from his own Jewish perspective, the only disquieting aspect of the nuns' presence was the desire to name the convent after Edith Stein which could indeed be interpreted as proselytizing. However, the Carmelite Order is purely contemplative and has no evangelic function within the Church – a fact confirmed by the instant withdrawal of the intended name by the nuns when they understood the implications. Krajewski regarded this as a compromise which he hoped would encourage Jewish circles to act in a similar vein. He pointed out that the building in which the convent was located had been in existence long before the camp was created, that it was outside Auschwitz and not Birkenau, and that the Poles have a right to pray for the hundreds of thousands of their own victims who also perished there. Jewish appeals for silence on the site ignore the fact that the predominantly Jewish Birkenau has remained unchanged and therefore silent, while Auschwitz already has a museum with all the accompanying paraphernalia catering for visitors. The absence of the Church in a place bursting with secular activity is unnatural. 'Moreover, it is in fact religious undertakings, including the Carmelite convent, which stand a chance of transforming this tourist centre into something more appropriate – a centre for pilgrimage.' According to Krajewski, the prayers at Auschwitz could have constituted the best incentive for the Church to acknowledge its guilt before the Jews.

Krajewski's article, published in *Tygodnik Powszechny* was the first public discussion of the problem in Poland. His views were supported by a prominent exponent of Polish-Jewish reconciliation, Józef Lichten. Born in 1906 into an assimilated and prosperous Jewish family in Warsaw, a lawyer and a Polish diplomat, after 1945 the initiator of the first Catholic-Jewish dialogue in the United States, between 1963–65 he represented the Anti-Defamation League of B'nai B'rith at the sessions of the Second Vatican Council. Lichten's study of the links between Christian belief – especially concerning deicide – and anti-semitism is said to have contributed greatly to the formulation of the theological position on the Jews in the encyclical *Nostra Aetate*, issued by John XXIII. After the Council, Lichten represented the Anti-Defamation League at the Vatican and had frequent contacts with Paul VI and John Paul II who awarded him the highest papal honour, Knight Commander of the Pontifical Order of St Gregory the Great. He was one of the most important mediators between the two communities. In his article *Z Pełnym uznaniem*, he supported Krajewski's position regarding the convent.

Some Jewish circles interpreted the timing of Krajewski's article as linked to Papal activities. On April 14, 1986, while Cardinal Glemp was expanding on his views to the Jewish delegation in Paris, Pope John Paul II visited the Great Synagogue in Rome where he attended a prayer service and gave a sermon. In it, the Pope stressed that the Church rejected all manifestations of anti-semitism and reminded the congregation of what he said during his visit to Birkenau in 1979. The Pontiff, in a clearly understood allusion, condemned in the name of Christianity all anti-Jewish acts perpetrated in the past by Christians: 'The Church deplores the hatred, persecutions, and displays of anti-semitism directed against the Jews at any time, and by anyone. I repeat, by anyone.' He also confirmed his desire to conduct and 'deepen the dialogue in loyalty and friendship, in respect for one another's intimate convictions, taking as a fundamental basis the elements of the revelation which we have in common as a "great spiritual patrimony"'. This visit, the first ever by any Pope to a synagogue, was universally applauded by Jewish communities as a highly significant, symbolic gesture. The Roman newspapers commenting on the Pope embracing the Chief Rabbi of Rome, Elio Toaff, proclaimed it to be 'an historic embrace that has waited 2000 years'.

The Polish Catholic Press Breaks the Story

The article by Turowicz, published in the same issue of *Tygodnik Powszechny* as that of Krajewski, was an attempt to begin such dialogue within Poland and to explain the problem to Poles who were largely ignorant of the issues and of the nature of Jewish objections. Turowicz admitted that the outbreak of the controversy over the convent came as a complete surprise to Polish Catholics 'to none of the initiators of the project had it occured that it might provoke such a reaction. Admittedly, we, the Catholics, may not have taken sufficiently into account the justified and understandable sensitivity of the Jewish community on the subject.' Turowicz tried to explain at length the difference between the fate of Poles and that of Jews during the war which had been suppressed by the post-war Communist government, and by nationalistic Poles, so that the majority of the population have no notion of the uniqueness of the destruction of the Jews. He emphasized that for the Jews, history is divided into 'before Auschwitz' and 'after Auschwitz', a place which symbolizes for them 'total abandonment, complete solitude in the face of death, the passivity of other nations, witnesses to the destruction.' As such, the Jews have 'every right to regard Auschwitz as a symbol of destruction'.

Turowicz also pointed out that various attempts to deny, and falsify the Holocaust, made Jews suspicious of anything which might suggest a revision of the past. Catholics should therefore be respectful even if the Jews are oversensitive. The Poles should not regard the campaign against the convent as an 'anti-Catholic or anti-Polish conspiracy', although the Jews do not have an exclusive right to the camp. Auschwitz is a monument of Jewish destruction, but Oświęcim (the Polish name for the camp) 'is also a symbol of the martyrdom of the Polish people during the Nazi occupation.' Auschwitz should be a place where Poles and Jews could unite, despite the fact that the extermination of the Jews and the fate of the

Poles were not parallel. Auschwitz/Oświęcim are two respective symbols which should not divide the two communities.[12]

Turowicz, who is a personal friend of the Pope, and one of the most influential lay Catholics in Poland, made an appeal for the problem to be resolved through dialogue, which indeed soon took place. Theo Klein, a representative of French Jewry, conveyed through Cardinal Lustiger his willingness to open a dialogue with Cardinal Macharski. In July 1986, Cardinal Macharski himself made an unexpected three-day visit to Israel on the invitation of Teddy Kollek, Mayor of Jerusalem. There he visited Yad Vashem, the museum-memorial devoted to the destruction of European Jewry. It was subsequently reported that he professed to have gained a greater understanding of Christian, Polish, and Jewish relations, and expressed his desire for more formal dialogue.

Indeed, the Catholic and Jewish representatives soon agreed to meet in order to find a solution acceptable to both sides which would also favour dialogue between the Catholic Church and the Jewish people.

CHAPTER 4

Geneva

Jews and Catholics Meet in Geneva

The first such meeting took place on 22 July, 1986 in Geneva. The Jewish side was represented by the leaders of Italian, French, and Belgian communities. The Catholic side included cardinals from Poland, France, and Belgium and one Catholic layman. At the meeting, Cardinal Macharski agreed to stop the construction of the convent. The nave was not to be consecrated which suggested the provisional character of the building. In return, the Jewish side acknowledged the fact of Polish suffering during the war. The participants issued a common declaration which recognized Auschwitz and Birkenau as symbols of the extermination of six million Jews who 'died abandoned by an indifferent world'. The declaration also singled out the Poles, Gypsies, and Russian prisoners of war who were the other principal victims of Auschwitz and Birkenau and called for silent prayer for all of the above.

The spokesman for the Jewish delegation, Professor Ady Steg of the *Alliance Israélite Universelle*, in an introductory speech at the Jewish-Christian summit outlined the reasons for Jewish opposition to the convent. Apart from those which had already been voiced by various Jewish communities, he considered that the existence of the Carmel could be perceived as part of an attempt to appropriate the Holocaust, to repress and remove it, and by doing so to deny the culpability of the world. Commenting upon the debate about the precise location of the convent, Steg did not consider that the question of whether the convent was inside or outside the camp boundaries was relevant, but he focussed on the fact that the building was used by the Nazis to store, among other things, cans with Cyklon B gas which was used in the gas chambers. This gas has become the 'chemical symbol of the *Shoah*'.[1]

The first meeting in Geneva could be regarded as the opening of the dialogue between Christian and Jewish communities. Protests against the convent continued in the following months, as did attempts to establish some basic facts. Thus Rabbi Norman Solomon, in an article published in *Christian–Jewish Relations*, reminded the readers that Jews were not the only victims and, using an old aerial photograph of the camp, proved that the wall which separates the convent from the rest of the camp had always been there, and had not been built after the war as some Jewish circles had suggested. At the same time, he confirmed that, as a site on the World Heritage List, the preservation of Auschwitz is covered by the UNESCO Convention. Because of this, the responsibility for the fate of the convent rested, according to him, with the Polish government and 'certainly not upon the Church who acquired the "theatre" from the government only in 1984, presumably on the basis that the government considered it "outside the camp"'.

Despite the fact that over a year had passed since the beginning of Jewish protests, some basic facts still had to be explained. It is a testimony to the level of ignorance of the general public that Rabbi Solomon found it necessary to reassert that there had been non-Jewish victims of Auschwitz-Birkenau.[2]

Jewish pressure on the Church continued especially in Belgium where various appeals and declarations were being issued. The convent was seen as an important aspect of Christian-Jewish relations in general. As one Belgian declaration put it 'there will be neither peace nor tranquility as long as a shadow in the shape of the cross falls on the immense field of our unappeasable sorrow'. *Regards* published a special issue largely devoted to 'Jews and Christians after Auschwitz'.[3] Some Jews expressed the sentiment that the Church would not honour the commitments made in Geneva, but most Jewish leaders were optimistic and took a positive view of the Church's reaction. Some informal high-level meetings between the two sides took place, keeping the dialogue alive.

The Second Geneva Meeting Brings Agreement

On 22 February 1987, a second meeting took place in Geneva attended by: Theo Klein (President of *Conseil Representatif des Juifs de France*), Rabbi Sirat (*Grand Rabbin*, France), Markus Pardes, Professor Ady Steg, and Tullia Zevi (President of the Union of Italian Jewish Communities), all of whom had participated in the first meeting. Also present were Dr E.L. Ehrlich (European Delegate of B'nai

B'rith), Sam Hoffenberg (Delegate of B'nai B'rith at UNESCO), Dr Gerhart M. Riegner (co-Chairman, World Jewish Congress Governing Board), and Professor Georges Schneck. On the Catholic side were Cardinals Danneels (Archbishop of Brussels), Decourtray (Archbishop of Lyons), Lustiger (Archbishop of Paris), and Macharski, together with Jerzy Turowicz, Fr Musiał SJ, and Kazimierz Jan Górny (Auxiliary Bishop of Cracow).

During the meeting, which was chaired by Cardinal Decourtray and Theo Klein, Professor Steg acting again as a Jewish spokesman, conceded that there were far fewer Jews killed in Auschwitz than in Birkenau, but insisted that it was Auschwitz which remained the symbol of the destruction of the Jews and thus had to be accepted as such: 'And if Auschwitz has become the symbol of the Holocaust it is not *we* who have decided this: a symbol does not decree itself. It is the universal conscience which has seen in Auschwitz, and not in Birkenau, Treblinka or Sobibór, the place of the Jewish catastrophe.'[4] He claimed that the memory of the Poles killed at Auschwitz had to be honoured elsewhere, in the numerous churches, convents, and monuments erected all over Poland.

As Theo Klein stated later, the Catholic delegation arriving in Geneva had only one choice – to support the Carmelites or to continue the dialogue with the Jews.[5]

The Geneva Declaration

Faced with this alternative, the Church agreed to a compromise. Both sides issued a declaration signed by all participants (bar one):

> Having recalled the terms of the declaration of 22 July 1986 recognizing that Auschwitz remains eternally the symbolic place of the *Shoah* which arose from the Nazi aim of destroying the Jewish people in a unique, unthinkable and unspeakable enterprise.
>
> In the common desire to ensure respect for the memory of the dead in the places where Nazi crimes were perpetrated and, in particular, where the extermination of the vast majority of the Jewish communities of Europe was carried out.
>
> Recalling this dramatic period which also demands profound respect for and devout meditation upon the sufferings of the Polish nation at this time and in this place.

The undersigned are in solemn agreement in what follows:

1 The Catholic delegation declares that, taking a stronger sense of its responsibilities towards future generations, it undertakes to embark upon a project, to be carried out by the European churches, which will create a centre of information, education, meeting and prayer. This centre will be established outside the area of Auschwitz-Birkenau camps. To this effect steps have already been taken to involve the Catholic Churches in Europe and all other Churches likely to support this project. Its aims will be:

(a) to encourage exchanges between the European Churches on the subject of the *Shoah* and also on the martyrdom of the Polish people and other peoples in Europe during the totalitarian horror throughout the war of 1939–1945

(b) to combat disinformation and trivialization of the *Shoah,* and to combat revisionism

(c) to receive groups of visitors to the camps to complete their information

(d) to encourage colloquia between Jews and Christians

2 The establishment of this centre is the continuation and the consequence of engagements undertaken at the meeting of 22 July 1986 in Geneva. It implies that the Carmelites' initiative of prayer will find its place, confirmation and true meaning in this new context, and also that due account has been taken of the legitimate sentiments expressed by the Jewish delegation. There will, therefore, be no permanent Catholic place of worship on the site of Auschwitz and Birkenau camps. Everyone will be able to pray there according to the dictates of his own heart, religion and faith.

3 The Catholic delegation specifies that Cardinal Macharski is to oversee the implementation of this project, while the bishops of other countries undertake to raise the means for its realization within the period of 24 months. Cardinal Macharski will keep President Theo Klein informed about progress in the realization of this project.

4 The Jewish delegation takes note of the foregoing undertakings made by the Catholic delegation.

5 Both delegations are conscious of having conducted their

dialogue in a common desire to emphasize the uniqueness of the *Shoah* within the tragedy of the Hitler era which had so cruelly affected the peoples of Europe and in particular the Polish people, and to ensure respect for the identity and the faith of every man and woman, both in their lifetime and at the place of their death.[6]

Jewish Reactions to the Geneva Agreement

The Jewish side reacted very positively to this declaration and some Jewish participants remarked that the outcome must have had the backing of the Pope. The Catholic side – which made all the concessions – refrained only from accepting the boundaries of the camp as defined by the Polish government's application to the UNESCO World Heritage List. The reason for this was that the Polish Church did not want to be bound by any agreements made solely by the Communist Government. This rejection was one of the reasons why Sam Hoffenberg refused to sign the final declaration. He feared that the Polish Church would try to redefine the boundaries instead of moving the convent, that it was playing for time and generally had bad intentions, and that the Jews would not approve of the ecumenical centre anyway.[7]

The *Jewish Chronicle* expressed fears that if the Jewish community did not help to raise funds to relocate the nuns the idea of the new centre could flounder. It speculated that a 'moving letter' written by the Study Centre for Christian-Jewish Relations (Sisters of Sion) in London, to the Carmelite Convent was a vital factor in the decision. The letter from the Christian group expressed distress at the erection of the convent and pleaded that Jewish anguish should be heeded.

The Polish Government Gives Its Approval

The Polish government gave written assurances in February 1987 in which it approved the relocation of the convent and the creation of a new ecumenical centre. On 31 December 1987, Władysław Loranc, the Polish Minister for Religious Affairs (from 1987), wrote a letter addressed to Gerhart Riegner, Co-Chairman of the Governing Board of the World Jewish Congress, declaring the Polish government's

47

very positive attitude towards the project of erecting a centre of information, education, meeting, and prayer at Oświęcim, outside the territory of the Auschwitz-Birkenau camps. In his letter he expressed the hope that 'the implementation of that initiative will definitely put an end to the disagreement that has arisen between the Roman Catholic Church and the Jewish organisations with regard to the places of worship on the grounds of the Auschwitz-Birkenau camps.' Loranc informed the World Jewish Congress that the Voievod of Bielsko-Biała and representatives of the Archbishop of Cracow had reviewed possible suitable locations for the centre which were retained pending a final choice. Riegner told the press that Church representatives in Poland claimed that they could not act without government's permission. Minister Loranc promised to intervene and his letter was the result. The World Jewish Congress expressed its hope that 'the Vatican and Church authorities would now move to carry out the Geneva agreement and avoid additional strain on relations'. Further meetings between Jewish organisations and the Polish government took place in April 1988 during the week-long commemoration of the 45th anniversary of the Warsaw Ghetto uprising. Minister Loranc disclosed that the government had offered the convent the choice of three specific sites outside the area. The Church authorities were in the process of considering two of these locations and were expected to make a final choice within two or three months. Once again, the general public remained largely unaware of these negotiations. This was partially due to the fact that the government was conducting a two-tier policy in respect of Jewish matters. While courting Israel and various Jewish organisations in the United States and elsewhere, it did not encourage discussions about the Jews within Poland itself. Jewish topics which had been taboo since the anti-semitic campaign 1967–69 were an embarrassment for the authorities who preferred to maintain close control over any contacts with the Jews, especially those living abroad. The position of the government on Jewish issues was made worse by its desire to increase its popularity (which by 1987 was very low indeed) by upholding national traditions and myths, while at the same time trying to avoid antagonising Jewish public opinion abroad. Polish communists, who viciously attacked various 'bourgeois' patriotic images until 1956, decided to play the nationalist card to gain popularity. As a result the government was not interested in informing the Poles in any detail of its contacts with the Jews or the Israelis.

Unbridgeable Differences Overlooked

The activities undertaken by the Polish government after the meeting in Geneva ran parallel to those of the Church. Cardinal Macharski explained the background and significance of the Geneva Declaration to a Catholic audience in a broadcast on Vatican Radio on 25 February 1987. In it he explained that in 1971 Karol Wojtyła, then Cardinal Archbishop of Cracow, had already expressed a desire to build a church in Auschwitz as 'a monument of the martyrdom of nations at Auschwitz'. Cardinal Wojtyła had approached the bishops of the countries whose citizens were victims of the camp. During the Synod of Rome, on the eve of the beatification of Fr Kolbe, Wojtyła had offered a relic to the bishops present – earth from Birkenau containing the ashes of those murdered there. According to Macharski, by beatifying one victim, the millions of other victims were also honoured. He also stated that this action pointed to the only guarantee against a repetition of the tragedy of Auschwitz. This guarantee was the 'love of Christ, stronger than hatred and all evil'. Although the Jewish community was aware of the interview given by Macharski, this phrase seems to have escaped their attention.

It is inconceivable that any Jew would look to Christian love as a guarantee against genocide, or that they would accept the commemoration of Fr Kolbe's sacrifice as an appropriate way to honour the largely Jewish victims of the camp. The message of Macharski, which was partially reported by an organ of the World Jewish Congress, was well-received but the theological gap between Christianity and Judaism as revealed by this interview could not be more obvious. Despite all the good will shown by Macharski, there were unbridgeable differences between the *Weltanschauung* of a prince of the Church and that of an Orthodox Jew. These differences also played a considerable role in the continuing controversy, since the average believers of both religions had considerable difficulty in understanding the sophisticated positions of their respective religious representatives.

The plan to build a church at Auschwitz had matured over several years and included annual meetings between German and Polish Christians at Auschwitz during which the bishops prayed together at the 'wall of death', the place of execution of many prisoners. The Pope's visit to the camp in 1979, the canonisation of Maximilian Kolbe in 1982 as a 'martyr of Auschwitz', and the foundation of the convent in 1984 were a part of this process. This showed that there was a 'religious dimension to the tragedy in the camp of Auschwitz' which would finally be acknowledged permanently by the establishment of the ecumenical centre. Macharski stressed the universal message which was to be conveyed to the world:

> The memory of the millions of innocent victims of hatred should not be allowed to fade. And this memory is threatened: by apathy, over-familiarity, a lack of information, and falsifying the truth about the death camps. It is not enough to visit the camp, all need to reflect deeply, and believers must also pray. The warning that genocide could be repeated anywhere in the world should not be ignored. All believers should witness that it is possible to live in a world of freedom, justice and love. Such is the purpose of the centre of prayers, studies, information, meetings in Auschwitz.'[8]

The Poles Learn About Geneva II

The Poles learned about the second Geneva meeting from an article written by Fr Stanisław Musiał, the Polish Jesuit who participated in the negotiations, and a member of the Polish Episcopate's Commission for Dialogue with Judaism. In his commentary to the meeting in Geneva, he stated that there were two nations for which Auschwitz constituted 'a particularly sinister symbol of death' – Jews and Poles. 'It can never be sufficiently emphasised that the fate of the Jews during the last war was incomparably worse than that of any other nation. Never before in the world's history had there been a crime of such evil'. Coming from a Polish clergyman, this represented a notable change of tone.

Fr Musiał also tried to explain the symbolic importance of the camp for both the Jewish and the Polish communities and noted that the Geneva Declaration had 'the merit of reminding us of the martyrdom of the Polish people during the last war by referring to it three times in the text.' This reference was clearly meant to pacify public opinion in Poland which the author had probably anticipated would be against the concessions made by the Church in Geneva. This is why Fr Musiał claimed that the meeting in Switzerland had been devoted not so much to the presence of the convent, but to the development of the project of the new 'Catholic Centre for meetings, reflection and prayer' which would also be open to the Jews. As events have shown, his fears about Polish reactions were well founded. The statements issued after Geneva constituted the first attempt to explain the issues to the Polish public. However the problems involved were too complex to be adequately explained in a mere handful of articles. General Polish ignorance about Jewish matters remained almost complete, and this lack of knowledge, which the Church itself did little to rectify, was to haunt the Church for the next few years and make it difficult to implement the decisions taken in Geneva.

Fr Musiał stressed the need for the new Centre to encompass the spiritual element. This would be achieved with 'the support of prayer in an institutionalized form provided by a contemplative convent. The role of the Carmelite convent should be seen in this context. The convent will continue to exist in Auschwitz [meaning of course in the area, but outside the boundaries of the camp] in an atmosphere – we hope – of tranquillity and silence, as befits its vocation'.[9]

The first discordant voices from the Catholic side were soon heard. In February 1987, Cardinal Glemp, the Primate of Poland made a statement commenting on the Geneva Declaration in which he stated that although he fully approved of the idea to create a new 'multi-faith institute', he did not consider 'the matter to be closed' and said that the dialogue between the two sides 'must be continued'.

In the meantime, the problem of the convent passed into the background and was replaced by the most important Polish debate about the Holocaust for over 40 years. The row has subsequently been referred to as the Błoński controversy.

CHAPTER 5

Polish Responsibilities for the Holocaust?

In 1943, Czesław Miłosz, the Lithuanian poet, and winner of the Nobel Prize for Literature in 1980, writing in Polish, wrote two poems related to the fate of the Jews in occupied Warsaw – 'Campo di Fiori' and 'A Poor Christian Looks at the Ghetto'. Both provided the pretext for a complicated moral and ethical discussion based on detailed and extensive analysis of the poems on the part of a literary historian and critic, Professor Jan Błoński, in an article entitled 'The Poor Poles Look at the Ghetto' (*Tygodnik Powszechny*, 11 January 1987). Błoński's goal was to re-examine the moral issues involved in coming to terms with the Polish-Jewish past and especially with Polish attitudes towards Jews during the Second World War. For decades, certain problems regarded as sensitive in Poland had not been publicly debated despite their effect on Poland's image abroad. The most crucial of these was the problem of Polish-Jewish relations during the War, which included the behaviour of the Poles towards the Jews, the question of moral co-responsibility for the fate of the Jews and, related to these, the problem of the Poles' self-image. Poles travelling abroad are used to hostility and accusations of 'eternal Polish anti-semitism' and collaboration with the Germans in the extermination of the Jews. Issues like these had not been analysed or examined in the media, but large sections of the intelligentsia had been aware of their existence and had felt uneasy about them. Błoński was the first person to attempt to address the issue directly in the press, albeit via literary rather than historical analysis.

Miłosz, says Błoński, often spoke in a 'perplexing' way about 'the duty of Polish poetry to purge the burden of guilt from our native soil', which is 'sullied, blood-stained, desecrated'. Błoński analyses these words and comes to the conclusion that Miłosz is not referring to the Polish or German blood spilt during the Second World War, but to Jewish blood:

> the genocide which – although not perpetrated by the Polish nation – took place on Polish soil and which has tainted that soil

for all times. That collective memory which finds its purest voice in poetry and literature cannot forget this bloody and hideous defilement. It cannot pretend it never occurred.

This opening sets the tone for Błoński's entire argument which was not a legal or historical discourse, but an ethical and moral one. Błoński's emphasis was on Christian morality and the collective memory of the Polish nation which identifies itself with common traditions. A clear distinction is made here between *guilt* and *moral responsibility*.

Błoński insisted that the common duty of the Poles which stems from Miłosz's poem was to examine and address the issues stored in this common memory. One of them is the fate of the Polish Jews who departed forever: 'Our country ... is a home which is built above all of memory; memory is at the core of our identity. We cannot dispose of it at will, even though as individuals we are not directly responsible for the actions of the past. We must carry it within us even though it is unpleasant or painful. We must also strive to expiate it.' The language of Błoński, full of religious and ethical references, likened the Jews to Abel. Their blood seeped into the soil and into the walls of the home which they shared with the Poles. Abel's blood did indeed enter into the Poles and their memory. To 'purify after Cain', Poles must remember Abel, cleanse themselves, see themselves 'in the light of the truth', otherwise their country and they themselves would remain tainted. Błoński acknowledged this to be a particularly difficult task and as an instance of this he quoted 'Campo di Fiori'. In this poem, written during the Warsaw Ghetto uprising, Miłosz compares the scenes in Warsaw to those on Campo di Fiori in Rome, the square on which Giordano Bruno was burned. The poem refers in particular to the merry-go-round built by the Germans in Krasiński Square in Warsaw next to the wall of the ghetto just before the uprising. The crucial passage describes the scene after the outbreak of the uprising:

> Sometimes the wind from burning houses
> would bring the kites along,
> and people on the merry-go-round
> caught the flying charred bits.
> This wind from the burning houses
> blew open the girls' skirts,
> and the happy throngs laughed
> on a beautiful Warsaw Sunday.
>
> [translated by A. Gillon]

Miłosz compares this with the burning at the stake of the Italian philosopher Giordano Bruno, amongst the oblivious Roman crowds, on the orders of the Inquisition, and reflects on the loneliness of the dying and the inhumanity of the witnesses. 'Campo di Fiori', translated into many languages (including Hebrew), was often taken as an accusation, as proof of the hostile indifference of the Poles. Błoński, however, quotes Miłosz years later as wondering

> Whether there really was such a street in Warsaw. It existed, and in another sense it did not. It existed, because there were indeed merry-go-rounds in the vicinity of the ghetto. It did not because in other parts of town, in other moments Warsaw was quite different. It was not my intention to make accusations.

The poem written, according to Miłosz, as an 'ordinary human gesture', saved, as someone put it, 'the honour of Polish poetry', which otherwise ignored the event. Błoński's analysis of the poem served to illustrate why it is so difficult for the Poles to come to terms with their Polish-Jewish past. In a dialogue which was a composite of conversations held over the years by Poles travelling abroad and encountering criticism – of Polish anti-semitism, intolerance, bad treatment of the Jews before the Holocaust, lack of help for the Jews during the Holocaust, pogroms after the War – Błoński summarizes the arguments on both sides and finds them very unsatisfactory and frustrating. Nor does he approve of the historical debates which tend to use the same arguments, only better documented. He feels that the key to understanding and overcoming the problem is to be found in that other war-time poem by Miłosz 'A Poor Christian Looks at the Ghetto'.

Here Miłosz speaks of the destruction of a city, the ghetto, where everything collapses in flames and only the trampled earth, full of human bodies, remains. A guardian mole appears surveying the dead. The mole, for Błoński, has the features of a Jew poring over the Old Testament, 'reading the great book of the species'. The poet lies among the dead, as if buried, afraid of the mole:

> This mole burrows underground, but also underneath our consciousness. This is the feeling of guilt which we do not want to admit. Buried under the rubble, among the bodies of the Jews, the 'uncircumcised' fears that he may be counted among the murderers. So it is the fear of damnation, the fear of Hell ... This Christian feels fearful of the fate of the Jews but also –

muffled, hidden even from himself – he feels the fear that he will be condemned.

This condemnation will come, not from the people, says Błoński, but from 'the mole ... who *may* condemn him', from the 'moral conscience ... of the poor Christian. And he would like to hide from this mole-conscience, as he does not know what to say to him'.

Herein lies the hidden key to Polish attitudes towards the Polish-Jewish past according to Błoński: 'The fear that one might be counted among the helpers of death'. Poles discussing the past with Jews try to explain or minimize the importance of events showing them in a bad light. They feel, however 'that not everything is as it should be'. The Poles are afraid of accusations, but these must be faced and answered in an honest way. They cannot forget or take a defensive stance, but must face the question of responsibility in a totally sincere manner. Here again it has to be stressed that Błoński refers to moral responsibility, and not to guilt, which he denies attaches to the Poles as a nation.

This point was not sufficiently understood by most commentators who, as Błoński subsequently remarked,

> had shown themselves incapable of understanding what moral responsiblity is. They only understand criminal responsibility: whoever is caught is guilty. Poles were not guilty of aiding the killings. In Poland, perhaps, the Germans had fewer direct helpers than anywhere else ... but the question is not one of accounting ... This is not the issue. The issue is that one can be co-responsible without co-operating – this was the idea of my article. To put it most generally, Polish responsibility is, in my opinion, centred on indifference, indifference at a time of the Holocaust.

Polish responsibility, according to Błoński, was also related to the fact that indifference often developed into enmity. If coexistence between different religions had been better in Poland (and elsewhere in Europe), the Nazi Holocaust would have been more difficult to plan and to carry out.

> Responsiblity, understood in this manner, the Poles share naturally with their neighbours, with the whole of Europe, with Christianity. They even, perhaps, share it with American Jews. I know what a tragedy it is for the Jews in the Diaspora, in America, who did not see what happened. I know, I well under-

55

stand, that tragedy. Yet it is more important to stress that we, unlike them, are not absolved by the fact that we did not know what was happening, first because we were on the spot and secondly because the Polish responsibility is greater by virtue of the fact that Jews lived on Polish lands, and we Poles should have known better, understood better than to make them a scapegoat for our own political and social difficulties.

In his original article, Błoński appealed to Poles to imitate the behaviour of the Catholic Church which admitted the wrongdoings of the past. If Christians condemned the Jewish nation, 'it was because Christians were not Christian enough'. The Catholic pronouncements stemming from the Second Vatican Council did not look for excuses or extenuating circumstances for Christian behaviour although such circumstances could be found. The Church spoke clearly 'about the failure to fulfil the duties of brotherhood and compassion. The rest is left to historians. It is precisely in this that the Christian magnanimity of such pronouncements lies.' Błoński demanded that Poles show a greater awareness of the problem, stop haggling about details best left to historians, admit their co-responsibility, and ask for forgiveness.

The Church Shows an Example

Błoński's appeal bore a certain similarity to the first attempts at Polish-German rapprochement in 1965. At that time, Polish bishops sent a letter to the German episcopate on the occasion of the coming millenium of Christianity in Poland in which, while referring to the common past, they declared 'we forgive and ask for forgiveness'. The letter was virulently attacked by the Polish government of Władysław Gomułka which in 1968–69 initiated an aggressive anti-semitic campaign resulting in the departure of about 20,000 Jews from Poland. The Church's position, which was not universally approved by the population, was defended by Jerzy Turowicz and *Tygodnik Powszechny* on moral grounds. This exchange between the churches which later led to a breakthrough in Polish–German relations was undertaken in the same spirit as Błoński's appeal. It was obvious, however, that it was easier for Polish society to accept the Bishops' letter than to come to terms with Błoński's article. Forgiving the Germans required only magnanimity since German guilt in respect of the Poles was incomparably greater than any Polish guilt the other way. The situation is more difficult in respect of Polish-Jewish history. Poles found it difficult to be compared with the Nazis in any way, although Błoński distinguished between participation in the crime and shared responsibility for it. For him, the Polish responsibility was 'for holding back, for insufficient effort to resist'. He referred primarily to the absence of positive action: 'if only in the past we had behaved more humanely, had been wiser, more magnanimous, genocide would perhaps have been "less imaginable", would probably have been considerably more difficult to carry out, and almost certainly would have met with much greater resistance than it did.'

Blonski Under Attack

The debate provoked by Błoński's article raged for weeks in the pages of *Tygodnik Powszechny* and some other papers, completely overshadowing the first reports about the Auschwitz convent controversy. Ultimately, however, they were closely linked since the convent issue depended on the interpretation of symbols of the past and Błoński's debate was about the Poles coming to terms with common Polish and Jewish history during the war.

Błoński's stance was soon to be violently attacked by Władysław Siła-Nowicki, a prominent lawyer and close cousin of Feliks Dzierżyński (the founder and first commander of the All Russian Extraordinary Commission for Combatting Counter-Revolution, Speculation, Sabotage, and Misuse of Authority, popularly known as the *Vecheka* or *Cheka*, the precursor of the NKVD and KGB). Siła-Nowicki's formal experience of inter-religious matters was restricted to a short period before the war when he served as a civil servant in the Department of Religious Affairs in the Ministry of Religious Affairs and Public Education. During the war, he was a member of the Home Army (the main anti-Nazi underground organization fighting the Germans in occupied Poland. It was recognized by the Western Allies as part of the Polish Armed Forces and had a membership of around 300,000.). After the war he was also a member of an anti-communist political organization created by former officers of the elite unit of the Home Army, *WiN* (Freedom and Sovereignty), and of a Christian-Democratic Party – *Stronnictwo Pracy* ('Labour Party'). Arrested by the communists in 1947 and sentenced to death, the sentence was commuted to life imprisonment and he was released during the 'thaw' in 1956. From 1959, he worked as a barrister defending many political prisoners. In 1980–81 he was an advisor to Solidarity and present at the historic signing of the Gdańsk Accords on 31 August 1980. In the last years of the Communist Government, he surprisingly became a member of the Consultative Council to the State Council of the Communist Government – for decades his patriotic credentials were otherwise impeccable.

Siła-Nowicki's response to Błoński's article was prompted by his fears that it would serve 'as the affirmation and quintessence (unintended of course), of a virulent, anti-Polish propaganda campaign, conducted endlessly for dozens of years by the enemies not of the Government, nor the economic or political system or present-day Poland, but simply of the Polish nation.'[1] He regarded the article as a very dangerous and 'propagandistic enunciation', and particularly regrettable because it was written by an eminent specialist in literature, and appeared in a leading Catholic social-cultural Polish paper.

Siła-Nowicki's approach to the problem may be characterized as narrow, legalistic and historically selective. His article reads as an emotional and skilful exercise in apologetics, but not without some demagoguery. He did not share Błoński's sensitivity and accuses him of taking matters seriously which have little bearing on reality. He regards the rhetorical dialogue conducted by Błoński as 'a litany of imaginary charges and answers to them [which] may find approval with anybody hating Poland'. Siła-Nowicki also dismisses the 'extensive and complicated deliberation' on Miłosz's poems as 'totally irrelevant', arbitrary, and not borne out by the evidence. He was clearly afraid about the damage the publication of Błoński's article might do to the image of Poland abroad. In this he was partially correct because most foreign journalists misunderstood, over-simplified, and distorted Błoński's message, which they took to be an admission that the Poles were guilty of genocide, an imputation strenuously denied by the author. Siła-Nowicki's response was constructed almost like a legal brief and his stance was that of nationalist apologetics: there was no virulent anti-semitic propaganda before the war, there was no moral savagery whatsoever during the war; Poles have nothing to be ashamed of and no nation in Europe can lecture them about their moral duties. The situation in Poland was harsher than in any other occupied country and nothing more could have been done. Siła-Nowicki allows no room for doubt: 'I am proud

of my nation's stance in every respect during the period of occupation, and in this I include the attitude towards the tragedy of the
Jewish nation. Obviously, the attitudes towards the Jews during that
period do not give us a particular reason to be proud, but neither are
they any grounds for shame, and even less for ignominy. Simply, we
could have done relatively little more than we actually did.'

Siła-Nowicki accuses Błoński of using the language of slanderers,
of deadly enemies of Poland, condemning savagery without acknowledging suffering or heroism. Błoński does not have the right,
he continues, to speak in the name of society, 'to lecture and
thunder'. If he is afraid of condemnation, this is not the feeling of
Siła-Nowicki and 'millions of Poles'.

Siła-Nowicki's article was often historically inaccurate and sometimes muddled. It contained praise of the Jewish nation for its
achievements, perseverance, strong identity and unity. It also spoke
negatively, however, about Jewish capitalists, separateness, passivity
during the war, and lack of resistance against the Germans. Parts of
his article can only be described as insensitive, chauvinistic, and
prejudiced. He disapproved of anti-Jewish measures at some Polish
universities before the war, such as the *numerus clausus* limiting the
number of Jews in higher education (a form of ethnic quota system),
or 'the ghetto benches', the enforced separation of Jews at university
lectures introduced in some places at the end of the 1930s, but con-
siders it appropriate to compare those measures with the much
worse situation which existed at the time in Nazi Germany. He does
not seem to realise the implications of such a comparison. He appor-
tions part of the blame to the Jewish side because a disproportionate
percentage of Jews wanted to enter universities: 'for me it is natural
that society defends itself against a numerical domination of its intelligentsia – pronounced especially in the medical or legal professions – by an alien intelligentsia. The coexistence of nationalities
must preserve a certain balance.'

Polish Jews: A Nation within a Nation?

This view illustrates one of the central problems in Polish-Jewish
relations – that of separateness. The Jews lived in Poland side by
side, rather than together with the Poles, and therefore many Poles
could and did regard them as a nation within a nation. The description of the Jewish community, which had lived in Poland continu-

ously for 800 years, as 'alien' can be understood only in such a context. The problem of achieving full civic equality was not restricted to Poland – it is enough to mention the position of Catholics in Wilhelmine Germany, Jews and Catholics in Victorian England or, more to the point, Jews in the United States where Ivy League universities such as Yale did not take any Jews until 1945. Jewish society in Poland included a numerically small but important intelligentsia – 56 per cent of physicians were Jewish, and so were one-third of all lawyers.

However, Poland was home to over three million Jews (about 10 per cent of the population) and the distinction between Catholic and Jewish Poles is false. Jews had no reason to assume that Poland was not their country since they were loyal citizens of the state. There were Zionists, of course, who wanted to emigrate to Palestine, but they were numerically few in comparison. In the thirties, the most popular of Jewish parties was the *Bund* (the Jewish Socialist Party) and the *Agudes yisroel* (traditional religious party) which did not advocate emigration.

While Błoński claimed that the Poles had taken Jews 'into our home, but we made them live in the cellar', Siła-Nowicki seemed to adopt the position criticized by Błoński that true Poles were 'only those Jews who are willing to cooperate in the attempt to stem Jewish influences in our society ... only those Jews who are willing to turn against their own kith and kin.'

Siła-Nowicki's article also came close to religious anti-semitism when he praised the succesful Jewish efforts to remain one nation despite centuries of living amongst others in the Diaspora: 'It is even possible to prove in the most scientific manner that in their veins flows only one per cent of the blood of those people who shouted "Hosanna to the Son of David" and then "Crucify Him! Crucify Him!": but their nation continues to exist.' While seemingly congratulating successful efforts to preserve Jewishness derived from kinship with the Biblical Hebrews throughout centuries of life in the Diaspora, Siła-Nowicki also hints at Jewish responsibility for Deocide – a view rejected by the Second Vatican Council in 1965.

These two contrasting attitudes, one characterized by its sensitivity and a moral-ethical perception of the past, and the other overly empirical and narrowly legalistic (together with the many shades of opinion which can be found in between), were also reflected in the Auschwitz controversy.

Błoński's article provoked a very lively response within Catholic intellectual circles, which discussed the most controversial aspects of Polish-Jewish relations publicly for the first time, marking the start of a re-evaluation of Polish-Jewish history from a different perspective. The religious factor played a particularly important role in the controversy since the issues were examined largely from the moral and Christian ethical standpoints. At the same time, the intelligentsia showed much more sensitivity than the Catholic public in general. It was this insensitivity combined with old-fashioned religiosity and nationalism which made it difficult to resolve the problem of the convent.[2]

CHAPTER 6

The Deadline Passes

The Poles Take No Action

Between 1987 and early 1989, no visible attempts were made on the Polish side to implement the agreement inherent in the second Geneva Declaration, nor to educate the Polish public in general or the inhabitants of Oświęcim in particular about the subject. Jewish visitors to Poland were alarmed that no specific steps had been taken by the Church during this period.

On 23 March 1988, Serge Cwajgenbaum, accompanied by Serge Klarsfeld, the famous Nazi hunter, spent a day of study at Auschwitz-Birkenau with 140 schoolchildren. The trip was sponsored by the French section of the World Jewish Congress. A delegation was allowed to talk with the Mother Superior's deputy who claimed that she had not been informed of any decision taken by the Episcopate about the convent in Auschwitz. On the contrary, she stated that since the nuns had lived in Oświęcim for 40 years they wished to remain there. The nuns reconstructed the building with great commitment because the fundamental reason for their presence in the camp was to pray for everyone, Jewish and Christian, who had been exterminated there. The Jewish delegation left the convent with the feeling that Cardinal Macharski had failed to communicate the decision about the transfer to the nuns who were therefore very reluctant to move.

Opposition Within the Polish Church

There were already indications in late 1987 that the implementation of the agreement was encountering significant opposition within the Polish episcopate. As one Catholic theologian who had been involved for years in Christian-Jewish dialogue in the United States noted, Cardinal Macharski was unable to persuade some members of the Polish Catholic hierarchy of the wisdom of the agreement.[1] The Polish public remained ignorant of the affair, although some eminent lay Catholics from Cracow drew Cardinal Macharski's attention to the fact that nothing was being done despite the passage of time, so that the issue was bound to re-emerge with a vengeance.

There has been much speculation as to why the Church was not anxious to act promptly in this matter. It is clear that Cardinal Macharski did not provide firm and decisive guidance to the officials in the Curia in his archdiocese. It has been suggested that although full of good will, and intending to fulfil the commitments stipulated by the Geneva Declaration, he seriously underestimated the strength of the opposition within the Curia and amongst the local population of Oświęcim. When he realised the degree of resistance, he decided not to push the issue or to use his authority to overrule objections, but played for time, hoping that passions would subside and that the issue would be resolved without confrontation. Because of the way the Church functions in Poland none of this became public knowledge.

The Polish Church is not generally known for its openness. Persecuted during the war by the Nazis, and throughout the post-war period by the Communist authorities, it has learned to protect itself by discretion carried to the point of secretiveness. Open debates within the Church which are a familiar practice in Western Europe are virtually unknown in Poland. There were, for instance, serious disagreements and differences of style between the late primate, Cardinal Stefan Wyszyński, and the then Cardinal Karol Wojtyła. These differences of opinion were known within the Church hierarchy, to prominent lay Catholics, and even to the Communist authorities who attempted, unsuccessfully, to play one Cardinal off against the other. The average Catholic, however, never had any idea that the Episcopate was not as fully united on all issues as it pretended to be in public, because no discussion ever took place in the open.

So Cardinal Macharski simply carried on the tradition. Macharski, who is an intellectual and a shy man, apparently dislikes controversies and prefers to settle problems behind the scenes in the best traditions of the Curia. It has also been suggested that various bishops were not happy about the speed with which he had agreed to the Jewish demands. Apart from disagreement over the principle of relocating the nuns, many people considered the two-year period suggested by the Geneva Declaration for the relocation to be totally unrealistic in Polish conditions. It has to be said that in the Poland of the late 1980s it was virtually impossible to build anything within two years. Some people who were informed about the problem considered it inevitable that the controversy would worsen because there was no chance that the new Centre would be completed by February 1989, as stipulated in Geneva.

As Filarski pointed out, there was also the question of the precise location of the convent. The Catholic delegation in Geneva refused to accept the Polish government's map submitted to UNESCO in support of the proposal to incorporate Auschwitz in the World Heritage List. Since the declaration stated that there would be 'no permanent Catholic place of worship on the site of Auschwitz and Birkenau camps', agreement as to precisely where the old theatre building occupied by the nuns was situated was of crucial importance. The original Polish line which was maintained by various people throughout the conflict, was that the convent was *outside* Auschwitz because it was divided from the camp by a wall. To the Polish participants at the Geneva meeting, it must have been clear that this interpretation was rejected by the other participants but, as Filarski reported after his conversations in Poland, some clergymen were keen on the sophistry that if the convent could be proved to be located outside the camp, the Carmelites would not be bound by the Geneva Declaration to quit the building.[2] Even had such an interpretation of the letter of the final declaration been possible, it would clearly have contradicted its spirit. All attempts to pretend otherwise were bound to damage the Church and antagonize either the Jewish or the French and Belgian Catholic parties to the agreement.

Auschwitz: A Clash of Symbols

More importantly, it was the clash of Polish and Jewish symbols which the Geneva declaration failed to reconcile. As Fr Bernard Dupuy, secretary of the French Episcopate's Committee for Relations with Judaism, pointed out in the spring of 1988, although the historical facts might have been sorted out, this had not surmounted differences of image. 'The Carmelite nuns, Monsignor Glemp, and Cardinal Macharski, even today say: Auschwitz is a symbol of Polish martyrdom! ... Even those Polish Catholics who are well-disposed do not appreciate what kind of symbol Auschwitz is for the Jews.'[3] Filarski has a point when he suggests that the Polish Church has generally been slower than some Western churches to follow the new Vatican line on relations with Judaism. The Polish Church has for a very long time been a defender of national symbols and at the same time a propagator of the slogan: 'to be a Pole is to be a Catholic', which did so much damage during the inter-war period when 40 per cent of the Polish population was made up of ethnic minorities which were not Catholic.

Various lay Catholic intellectuals in Poland recognised the scale of the problem and considered that the Jewish arguments, which at that stage had not been much reported or explained, would not convince Catholic public opinion in Poland. The common response would have been that the Jews wanted to forbid the Poles to pray for their own dead on the site where they were killed, which happens to be on Polish soil. Some suspected an outburst of anti-semitic sentiment in the country. According to Filarski, the Mother Superior of Carmel told him in April 1988 that the Jews interpreted the Geneva Declaration in 'bad faith' by suggesting that the nuns ought to move. 'Carmelite prayers give the best guarantee that Auschwitz will not be forgotten and the Jews do not understand that they have allowed themselves to be manipulated by forces which want the world to forget.'[4] The Mother Superior apparently considered the whole controversy to be an anti-Polish affair in which the government was not ready to intervene forcefully because it lacked the sort of money the Jews possessed.

As Filarski noted, the Carmelite nuns were as badly informed as Polish society in general, since the Episcopate had kept them largely in the dark. He did not question the nuns' good intentions, but they regarded the Jews in a stereotypical and traditional manner which is full of mistrust. As far as Polish society was concerned, faced as it was in 1987–88 with a political, economic, and social crisis, the problem surrounding Auschwitz was not the main preoccupation.

Jewish Unease Intensifies

With the passage of time, Jewish unease about the lack of progress in relocating the nuns intensified. The Jewish community became convinced that the removal of the convent would not take place before the deadline of 22 February 1989 set in Geneva. There was an apparent lack of eagerness to discuss the issue on the Catholic side. It was reported that Cardinal Johannes Willebrands, the Vatican Secretary of State and head of the Committee for Relations with Judaism, failed to appear in late December 1988 for a meeting with Jewish officials in Paris to discuss the convent. Rabbi Wolfe Kelman, chairman of the American Section of the World Jewish Congress, considered the non-implementation of the declaration signed in Geneva to be 'a very serious breach'. As a result of this breakdown in communication, the World Jewish Congress issued a resolution that its members would not participate in a Catholic-Jewish conference which was to take place in Zurich in February 1989 unless the Vatican ensured the removal of the convent. The conference in Switzerland was to initiate work on the history of anti-semitism in the Church. As the Jewish Telegraphic Agency reported, many Orthodox Jews considered it futile to hold any dialogue on theological matters with the Christians. At the meeting at which the resolution was passed, Rabbi Zvi Zakheim, a member of the World Jewish Congress, shouted 'I told you not to run to the *goyim*'.[5]

In January 1989, Dr Gerhard Riegner, a representative of the World Jewish Congress, in an interview with the International Catholic Press Agency, warned that unless the nuns vacated the convent there could be a complete suspension of relations between world Jewry and the Vatican. Accusing the Polish Church hierarchy of being insensitive, anti-semitic, and of living in the past, he declared himself of the opinion that 'the difficulties don't come from the Vatican. To the contrary, they come from the Polish Church, that has not yet achieved every new theology begun by Vatican II.' A proof of this could be found, according to Riegner, in the fact that there was no Polish version of the Vatican documents concerning relations with Judaism. He claimed that the reasons for this were first, 'the anti-semitic attitude of Polish society', secondly, because there were hardly any Jews still living in Poland and thus their lobbying power was minute, and thirdly because the Church in Poland lived as if 'in a fortress', defending its position against the Communists and 'not allowing any new trends, such as the new teaching of Vatican II, into Poland'. Riegner claimed that the removal of the nuns was a condition *sine qua non* for the construction of the Ecumenical Centre to begin.[6] Dr Riegner's severe warning was modified by a pronouncement made by Rabbi Mark Tannenbaum, the present Director for International Relations at the American Jewish Committee and Chairman of the International Jewish Committee on Inter-Religious Consultations and a highly influential Jewish leader engaged in consultations about the convent.

Rabbi Tannenbaum stressed that the immediate problem was to find an interim place to which the nuns could move. He agreed that the Jewish community should continue to put pressure on the Catholic side, but emphasised that in order for it to be effective it ought to take the form of 'reasonable and moderate statements that will support our allies and friends in the Vatican and the Polish Church, and not paralyze their ability to function by playing into the hands of our worst enemies among the Polish Catholic traditionalists. I think it is possible to find a constructive resolution, and we simply have to use prudence and wisdom to bring about that result.'[7]

The Polish Church Reaffirms the Geneva Declaration

The Polish Episcopate was so concerned about Gerhard Riegner's pronouncements that it felt compelled to issue a statement signed by Bishop Muszyński, the head of the Commission for Dialogue with Judaism which was subsequently published by *Przegląd Katolicki* (a Catholic paper) on 9 April. In it Muszyński emphasised that Cardinal Glemp and the entire Episcopate accepted the validity of Cardinal Macharski's project for the new centre of information, education, meeting, and prayer in Oświęcim. Countering Riegner's argument that the Polish hierarchy were slow to implement the changes in the Church's teaching with regard to Jews, following the Second Vatican Council, Muszyński pointed out that all important Church documents related to this matter had been translated into Polish and had been available in all dioceses throughout the country for many years. The Episcopate attempted to explain the delays in moving forward with the project by pleading 'objective difficulties'. As Muszyński said, it was not a matter of ill will, but partly of administrative formalities and partly of the historical associations surrounding Oświęcim and its symbolic meaning for the nation as a site of bloody Polish martyrdom. This innocuous document was in fact an important statement of the Episcopate's position which hinted at the difficulties facing the Church. By restating the point about the symbolic meaning of Auschwitz, the Episcopate admitted that there were people, either within the Episcopate, or amongst the Catholic population at large, who did not accept the Geneva declaration. Thus the Church felt unable to implement it and needed more time to resolve the issue.

Rumours Spread

Given the confusion which apparently existed within the Polish Church itself, it is not surprising that various official Church statements as well as contradictory rumours were circulating in Europe at this time. At the end of January 1989, Cardinal Decourtray of Lyon announced that the convent would be removed, but there were also rumours that the Polish Church would break the commitments which the Jewish side and the Western Catholic Church understood to have been agreed at Geneva.

Despite the fact that Jewish communities throughout the world displayed considerable interest in the problem of the Carmel, many individual Jews were not well informed about developments. The matter was complicated by the fact that many Jewish organisations operated largely in competition with each other. As a result the rumours about the refusal of the Polish Church to relocate the convent continued to circulate even after Cardinal Macharski had issued a statement on 24 January 1989 confirming that 'the new convent will be built away from the boundaries of the former Nazi camp, along with the interreligious centre for prayer and information. The convent will be constructed on separate grounds inside the new interreligious centre, so that it will be in the vicinity of the camp but well outside its boundaries.'

The same day, the Cardinal sent a telegram to Cardinal Lustiger in which he informed him that plans to build the Centre for Education, Information, Meetings, and Prayer in Auschwitz had entered 'the last phase of concretization. This applies equally to the location of the Centre opposite the so-called old theatre, as to the function and architectural design of the buildings of which it will consist. The realization of the project will begin immediately after the formalities have been completed.' He explained that the relocation of the sisters was to be done with 'selfless love and generosity, for the sake of tolerance and respect'. In a typically cryptic final statement he indicated that the old theatre building would also serve the same purposes as the Centre, though he was not specific as to what that would be.[8]

On 26 January, Cardinal Willebrands sent a telegram to Cardinal Macharski welcoming his statement and assuring him of his support. The announcement was also welcomed by Rabbi Tanenbaum who regarded it as a 'sign of good faith', and with more caution by the International Jewish Committee for Interreligious Consultations

(IJCIC), then headed by Rabbi A. James Rudin. The Committee decided to study the text of the pronouncements by both Cardinals and issued no statement. Unlike the Catholics with their clearly defined hierarchy of the Roman Church, the Jews are represented by a plethora of organisations, some of which often claim to speak in the name of world Jewry. The IJCIC consists of five separate groups – the American Jewish Committee, B'nai B'rith International, Israel Interfaith Association, Synagogue Council of America, and the World Jewish Congress – all of which have to agree to any official pronouncement. In general, the position of the Committee was that the Geneva Declaration provided the means for the resolution of the problem.

Clear indications about the problems encountered by Cardinal Macharski in the implementation of the declaration from Geneva came in his letter addressed to the inhabitants of Oświęcim.[9] In it, he largely repeated verbatim the message of his telegram to Cardinal Lustiger, but added significantly that he had written the letter as a response to rumours stating that the nuns were to be removed from Auschwitz. Macharski 'categorically declared' that the sisters would remain in Auschwitz, although they would fulfill their vocation in their own new cloister when it was built. It is obvious that by this stage the local clergy must already have informed him of the discontent felt by the local population. As it turned out, his assurances were not sufficient to appease the Catholics of Oświęcim since the Archdiocese did not make a sufficient effort to explain the reasons behind their decision about the convent.

The Church Fails to Meet the Deadline

On 14 February 1989, Cardinal Decourtray of Lyon who headed the Catholic delegation in Geneva, sent a long letter to Theo Klein who headed the Jewish delegation. He expressed deep regret that the Church would not be able to meet the deadline. Construction of the new cloister and of the Centre had not yet begun, and he appealed for more time. He understood that this could be interpreted as a failure to respect the undertakings made in Geneva. He emphasised however, that all of them would be honoured, as some of the problems had already been overcome. Decourtray outlined various difficulties – there were administrative complications involving the district authorities, and others arising out of Polish Catholic and national public opinion. The public had to be convinced that in honouring the agreement the Carmelites would not be wronged, and that the martyrdom suffered in this place by the Poles would not be denied. As he pointed out, 'It has been a momentous and extremely delicate task: one had at the same time to implement the agreement and to effect a change in [the] consciousness and mentality [of the public]'. He further stressed that the nuns had finally accepted the irreversible decision to relocate the convent which for him was of the highest significance. This acceptance was an act of obedience towards the Archbishop, taken in order to contribute to deepening relations between Jews and Catholics in the spirit of Vatican II. He asked for the nuns to be allowed to remain in the old theatre until 22 July 1989, after which they would be moved to other temporary premises.[10] Klein also received a private letter from the Father-General of the Carmelite Order in Rome, Monsignor Philippe Sainz de Baranda, promising that the nuns would be moved as soon as the building was ready, but not specifying any date. Klein, who represented all major French Jewish organizations at the time, responded that the relocation could not wait until 22 July, insisted that Cardinal Decourtray should ensure that temporary accommodation for the Carmelite nuns was immediately provided, and announced that Jewish-Catholic relations would be suspended until the matter was resolved. As the London *Jewish Chronicle* reported, Theo Klein considered Cardinal Macharski's attitude to be the main problem. He thought that neither the Polish Episcopate nor the nuns were ready to implement the provisions of Geneva II.[11]

Jewish Indignation Mounts

Dr Lionel Kopelowitz, president of the European Jewish Congress and of the London-based Board of Deputies of British Jews, also expressed regret, drawing attention to the fact that 'a signed agreement freely arrived at after long negotiations and discussions remains unfulfilled and that the convent is still at Auschwitz with an increased complement of nuns'. Kopelowitz considered this to be an affront to 'Jewish sensitivity on a most painful subject'.[12]

Protesting against the Church's inaction, the Brussels-based European Union of Jewish Students (EUJS) launched a letter-writing campaign to the Pope urging the immediate transfer of the nuns to temporary accommodation. Together with members of the Belgian Jewish Students Union, they occupied Sablon Catholic Cathedral in

Brussels. About 100 people, some of them Holocaust survivors, took part, including clergymen and members of the Council for Christians and Jews. Their action was condemned by the Jewish Central Consistory, the highest Jewish religious authority in Belgium.[13] This condemnation did not deter Melinda Simmons, the acting chairperson of the EUJS, from a bald statement of her views. In a letter to the *Jewish Chronicle* she concluded that almost all Jewish leaders were scared of the Catholic Church and were thus willing 'to allow a desecration of the victims of Auschwitz'. Showing a total ignorance of the Catholic faith, she claimed that the 'Carmelite nuns were praying over the bodies of Jews in order to "save" them by converting them to Catholicism' which she found 'intolerable and unacceptable'. The majority of Jewish leaders acted in a much more responsible manner, provoking Ms Simmons to ask bitterly 'Why does no one else agree with us?'.[14]

On the second anniversary of the Geneva meeting, 22 February 1989, Cardinal Macharski issued a pastoral letter in which he stated that plans to create the ecumenical centre were 'entering the phase of concretization' and that it would be built opposite the so-called 'old theatre', once formalities had been completed. Macharski's statement did not satisfy the Jewish community, various members of which expressed profound disappointment that 'the commitment undertaken by leaders of the Roman Catholic Church to representatives of the Jewish communities in Europe and solemnly spelled out in the "Geneva II" accord of February 22, 1987, remain unfulfilled', despite the passage of the full term prescribed by the Declaration. Rabbi A. James Rudin, Chairman of the IJCIC, complained that not a spade had been struck in the ground to build the new site for the nuns in the last two years. However, he also emphasised that the problem had a simple solution and that 'full and speedy implementation of Geneva II' would remove all the obstacles to the renewal of 'the fruitful and important dialogue with the Vatican'.[15] The general feeling amongst Jewish organisations was that it was the Polish Church that was being obstructive, while the French and Belgian Catholic hierarchy and the Vatican attempted, unsuccessfully, to mediate.

Raging Public Debate

An editorial in the *Jewish Chronicle* summed up Jewish feelings by saying that leading European Cardinals and the head of the

Carmelite Order acknowledged Jewish sensitivity on the issue but 'within the international Jewish community there is a sense of deep betrayal, even though the Vatican itself has been urgently pressing for the convent's removal. The Roman Catholic church in Poland, however, seems to be a law unto itself, despite the Pope's own close association with it.'[16] This editorial brought an angry response from a Polish reader of the paper, Teresa Rakowska, who totally rejected the view that Auschwitz could be 'just a shrine to the memory of the Jewish dead', emphasizing the symbolic nature of the place for the Poles. She considered Auschwitz to be a unique statement for Europeans about their civilization and its 'most besetting sin, racism'. She saw the place as a 'warning to mankind', but 'above all a symbol of the present – there is still racism, anti-semitism, death camps and killing fields – our civilization!' Because of this, Auschwitz, according to Rakowska, had to be more than a 'memory of the dead', it had to be a place where people atoned, 'praying and pleading for the dead that they may be at peace and their sufferings may not have been in vain. It is this work, of prayer and penance, that needs to be in evidence at this place and that is given expression in the Carmelite convent.'[17] Despite the fact that Rakowska claimed that these demands stem from a common biblical heritage, she obviously failed to understand that the Christian categories are in their essence very different to those which exist in Judaism. She did not understand that few Jews regard Christianity as a religion which shares their heritage. They are more likely to consider it to be a schism or a heresy in the name of which Jews were, for centuries persecuted throughout Europe.

Some of these points were mentioned in the letters published in response to Rakowska's statements in the *Jewish Chronicle*. The readers drew attention to the history of Church anti-semitism and the fact that the Nazis were nominally Christian, and suggested that a direct link existed between the anti-Jewish teachings of the Church – including the accusation of deicide and that Jews drank the blood of Christian children for ritual purposes which, although not officially approved by the Church hierarchy, was widely believed and disseminated by the lower clergy – and the genocide perpetrated to the accompaniment of almost complete silence from the Vatican and Pope Pius XII. On the whole the letters were highly critical of the Church and some, as Rakowska commented in her reply, contained 'a thinly veiled hatred of the Catholic Church for being the alleged culprit for what happened in the *Shoah*'.[18]

The Deadline Passes

A Cross Over Auschwitz

In March 1989, additional expressions of Jewish concern were declared after a 23-foot high cross was erected in front of the convent. Various Jewish delegations visiting the site were angered at the prospect of the new crucifix, which they described as 'a massive cross towering alongside the convent' which, according to them, 'symbolizes that the place belongs to the Catholics'. One such French-Belgian delegation which visited Auschwitz in March 1989 included a Belgian priest, Abbé Bernard, who brought with him a petition signed by 800 Belgian Catholics asking the nuns to leave. The nuns reportedly rejected the petition and refused the delegation entry to the convent.[19] This in itself is hardly surprising since the Discalced Carmelites are a strictly enclosed order with the minimum of contact with the outside world.

The first commentaries in the Polish press appeared in April of that year. After *Tygodnik Powszechny* published a statement by Cardinal Macharski explaining that the nuns would have to move as an expression of respect, a meeting attended by 700 inhabitants of Oświęcim, the town next to which the camp is located, passed a resolution which strongly protested against the decision to close the convent. Various local Catholics, including members of the Catholic Intelligentsia Club, expressed their concern and condemned the Polish Catholic press for not supporting their stance on the issue. An article by Leszek Konarski 'The Shadow of the Cross' in *Przegląd Tygodniowy* (16 April 1989), recounting these protests mentioned a letter signed by 1,375 inhabitants of the town of Oświęcim which *Tygodnik Powszechny* refused to print. In the letter they denounced 'intolerable pressures' which 'groups of Jews exerted in order to force the nuns to leave'. They also stressed that the convent was located outside the perimeter fence of the camp. The Jewish negotiators were well aware of these problems which Theo Klein referred to 'as internal Polish Church difficulties'. The letter was later printed in *Słowo Powszechne*, a nominally Catholic paper published by the pro-communist organization PAX which does not enjoy the official sanction of the Church. The letter described demands to oust the nuns from the convent as 'illegal' since the building had been legally leased. The article also condemned the Catholic press for being uncritical towards the Catholic delegation to the meeting in Geneva. The article quoted one of the sisters, Maria Magiera, who did not understand why their prayer 'profaned' the site. 'Prayer is not con-

73

nected with a place. Does it make any difference if we pray here or 100 yards further away on the other side of the street?' The nuns have nevertheless promised to obey any directive to move issued by the Holy See, although they thought that 'tolerance should be practised by everyone'. According to Konarski, there were a number of incidents at the convent and some threats were made during the celebration of the Warsaw ghetto uprising the year before – 1988. Since then the nuns have installed sturdy locks at their gate to discourage intruders. According to Konarski, the main issue was who should be allowed to pray for the victims of Nazi genocide. He accused the Jews of trying to monopolize Auschwitz as a Jewish cemetery, despite the fact that the majority of inmates of Auschwitz I, as opposed to the sub-camp Birkenau, were not Jewish.

Oświęcim's Catholics Reject Geneva II

Konarski described a meeting of a district organisation of victims of Nazi oppression. The participants issued an appeal in their name 'as Poles, Catholics, and victims of the war', protesting strongly against the 'liquidation of the convent, legally located with the full agreement of the authorities'. They stated further that 'The authorities should not change this decision regardless of how much they are pressurised to do so. The victims of war demand that the situation should be maintained as at present. We are determined to fight to keep the convent and ask the Catholic Church on all levels to support us in our efforts.'

This appeal had widespread local support which included not only the people of Oświęcim, but also the regional authorities. The local Catholics bombarded the Metropolitan Curia in Cracow with letters stressing that the Church's behaviour in the matter would cause irreparable damage to Polish-Jewish relations as far as the local population was concerned. The local inhabitants complained that their voices were completely ignored by Cardinal Macharski and large sections of the Episcopate, and were resentful towards the Catholic press which by and large ignored them, while presenting the point of view of Western Catholics and Jewish organisations. Much has been made of the different interpretation of the convent's precise location. Virtually no inhabitant of Oświęcim considered the convent to be part of the camp since it was visibly separated from it by a wall. It is almost certain that nobody in Oświęcim had ever seen the text of the

Polish government's application, with its accompanying map, submitted to the UNESCO World Heritage List, and so did not realise that the 'old theatre' which became a convent was included as part of the camp.

In the beginning of April 1987, the Polish Minister for Religious Affairs, Władysław Loranc, visited Israel. His week-long visit was the first by a Polish minister since 1967 when Poland followed in Soviet footsteps and broke off diplomatic relations with Israel. During his visit, Loranc admitted that a stalemate had developed in the dialogue between the Polish Church and the Jews on the issue of the convent, and he was afraid that if the situation deteriorated further, it would create 'a deep impasse between World Jewry and the Roman Catholic Church'. Responding to the Israeli journalists' questions, Loranc acknowledged the existence of anti-semitism in Poland which he said was no different from any other country, but also emphasised that there were also many philosemites, especially among the younger generation. He appealed to the world's press 'to be responsible and create the right climate ... this is not something one should play games with.' He also pointed out that the government was not involved in making the original agreement but that it would try to help to solve the problem by shifting the convent elsewhere.[20]

Moderating Voices Intervene

On 23 April 1989, *Tygodnik Powszechny* published an article devoted to the week of discussions about Auschwitz held annually by the Catholic Intelligentsia Clubs in which Andrzej Potocki appealed for the Poles to remember that despite the fact that several hundreds of thousands of Poles had perished in Auschwitz, the camp's main victims were Jews and it was the duty of Poles to recognize that they had on occasion been guilty of indifference, lack of compassion and neglect. Potocki attempted to explain that for those Jews who still live in Poland and, despite slights suffered, continue to feel Polish, their sense of religious identity is more important than their sense of national identity. For those Jews who live in the Diaspora, the common distinguishing feature is an everpresent wariness or fear. The Poles ought to understand what role Auschwitz played in the formation and continuation of this Jewish attitude.

Then as well as later there were some Jewish voices for whom the controversy was not particularly important. In a letter to the *The*

Times, Frank Pomeranz from London stated that, as a Jew, not only did he not object to the Church's honouring Edith Stein, but he considered it to be purely the Church's business, even if Sister Teresa Benedicta of the Cross was murdered because of her Jewishness in the eyes of the Nazis. Mr Pomeranz, rejecting the religious definition of who is a Jew, declared himself proud of the fact that some converted Jews had reached prominence in their fields. He recalled in particular Felix Mendelssohn and Heinrich Heine, recounting the following story about the latter: 'When, under pressure from religious zealots, the Tel Aviv municipal council refused to name a street after him, a number of indignant, though impeccably Jewish, literary men gathered in what was proposed should become Heinrich Heine Street and symbolically named it that.'[21] His voice could not however be considered typical or representative of the Jewish community. The particular difficulty surrounding Edith Stein with whom the Carmelite convent was clearly, if informally, linked, was that, although in the eyes of the Jewish religious authorities and those of the Catholic Church, she ceased to be Jewish after her conversion, she was nevertheless considered to be so under the Nazi Nuremburg Laws and was murdered as a Jewess. A further complication arose because some members of the Church could point out that although born Jewish, she consciously chose the Catholic faith and wrote numerous philosophical works about classical phenomenology, philosophical anthropology, and metaphysics, including a book on the philosophy of God entitled *Finite and Eternal Being* (*Endliches und ewiges Sein*). For the Jews, some of this suggested proselytizing triumphalism, despite the fact that by converting, Edith Stein, from a Jewish religious perspective, ceased to exist, as though she were dead. Regardless of this, large parts of the Jewish community are conscious that she died as a Jewess and resent the appropriation of her death, as they see it, by the Catholic Church.

The Carmelite Order Declares Its Position

The Polish Carmelite Order became visibly involved in the controversy in May 1989 when Fr Anastazy Gegotek, in an interview conducted by the Austrian Catholic Press Agency, stated on behalf of the Provincial of the Carmelite Order that the whole matter was a misunderstanding, because the gas chambers were located in Birkenau and not in Auschwitz, and that many Poles had been executed next to the theatre building. Fr Gegotek called the Jewish re-action very painful and incomprehensible, and he was also annoyed by Jewish protests on the site, especially by young Jews who distri-buted leaflets there. He considered Jewish complaints about the large cross in front of the convent as 'contradicting the spirit of dialogue' and added that the Church would not oppose the presence of a synagogue at Auschwitz.[22] Fr Gegotek's remark about a synagogue in the camp's grounds indicated the persistent lack of understanding between the two religious positions and the continuing insistence on parallelism on the part of Polish Catholics. This view did not take into account that the Jews might wish to honour the dead in a different way to that of the Catholic Church (the Jews would not build a synagogue in the grounds of what some considered to be a cemetery), and that the Jews objected in principle to being regarded as equal victims of the camp. This interview does not seem to be known in Poland, but Fr Gegotek's attitude and that of the Provincial of the Carmelite Order must have been known to the nuns and to the local Church.

Jewish opposition to this line of argument was articulated by the President of the World Jewish Congress, Edgar Bronfman who said that 'it is not only a matter of the Auschwitz convent, but the broader implications of historical revisionism in which the uniqueness of the Holocaust and the murder of the Jewish people is being suppressed'.[23] The resolution of the Congress passed in May 1989 called on the Pope to exercise his authority to ensure the prompt removal of the convent. The World Jewish Congress regarded the Pope's action as necessary. Numerous Jewish groups representing other organisations which planned to visit Poland at the time declared their intention to stage protest demonstrations in front of the Carmel. On 30 May 300 women from 27 countries representing the Women's International Zionist Organisation (WIZO) held a demonstration by the Convent. The protestors carried an Israeli flag and banners and placards with slogans such as 'Leave alone the memory of the millions of Jewish victims' and 'Remove the convent – Don't de-Judaize the Holocaust'.[24]

World Jewry Protests

Raya Yaglom, WIZO president, then had a meeting with Cardinal Macharski after which she stated that the Archbishop of Cracow admitted that he was not capable of implementing the Geneva undertaking. According to her, Cardinal Macharski 'justified this by repeating over and over that he had not expected the nuns to be so recalcitrant and that he had anyway received tens of thousands of letters from Polish Catholics who wanted the convent left where it was.' Yaglom announced that she left Poland with a clear feeling that 'there was a strong desire there, particularly in the Church, to de-Judaize the *Shoah* and turn it into a Christian Holocaust.' Her views on Poland were made clearer when, during a meeting with the Minister for Religious Affairs, she implied that it was not without reason that Hitler had chosen to locate the death camps on Polish soil.[25]

The Federation of Polish Jews in the United States representing the largest community of Polish Jews in the world, condemned the behaviour of the Polish Church hierarchy and 'the evasive attitude of the Vatican, which violates the letter and spirit of the 1987 accord'. The federation criticized the Polish government which, according to them, could not be absolved of its responsibility for the developments but in particular they singled out Cardinal Franciszek Macharski whom they considered to be 'chiefly responsible'. The Federation's members were convinced that the Church was prepared to establish numerous convents, chapels, and churches at Treblinka, Sobibór and other death camps whose victims were entirely Jewish.[26]

In June, Cardinal Macharski in communication with Archbishop Decourtray conveyed his understanding of Jewish anguish over the convent's presence in Auschwitz, but urged world Jewry to refrain from staging demonstrations at the site which provoked a knee-jerk defence of the sisters by the local people, and which could cause a rupture between Catholics and Jews which would be 'a great unhappiness'. In the meantime, the Polish government sent a number of communications to various Jewish leaders stating that the matter was entirely in the hands of the Church. On 4 June the weekly *Forum*, which prints selected articles from the foreign press, published an excerpt from an interview given by Bishop Muszyński to *La Croix*. In it Muszyński said that although the Episcopate had agreed to move the convent to another site, the agreement had not been accepted by the Catholic community at large, 'In Poland, the cross is a symbol of faith. For these people, to oppose the cross is synonymous with opposing the faith. We will have to explain that the cross and the place in which it is located are not the same thing.'

Polish Nationalism Emerges

The opposition to the removal of the convent was discreetly supported by an adviser to Cardinal Glemp, a member of the Primate's
Social Council (and also a member of a Communist front organisation compromised in the eyes of society, Patriotic Movement of
National Rebirth, *PRON*), Professor Maciej Giertych. According to
persistent rumours emanating from Warsaw, Giertych had been
linked with the anti-semitic propaganda spread by a group of priests
in a church in Solec in Warsaw, and with traditional, old-fashioned
Endecja circles (supporters of the pre-war, strongly anti-semitic
National Democratic Party, headed by Roman Dmowski). Professor Giertych had been known to make defiant statements, full of
nationalistic pride, opposing foreign interference in Polish affairs
over the convent. In 1988 he issued a statement criticising a document drafted by the Primate's Social Council, concerned with the
tolerance of divergent religious and philosophical outlooks. The
document suggested that Poland should aim to be a non-denomi-
national state where all religions are equally respected. Giertych
objected to this, stating that western-style liberalism is materialistic,
hedonistic, alien to the Polish tradition and leads to the collapse of
the family and to various social evils such as AIDS. The document
was later rejected by Cardinal Glemp.[27]

Professor Giertych heads the *Słowo i Czyn* [Word and Deed] organisation which is widely seen as chauvinistic, anti-semitic, with right-
wing totalitarian tendencies. On 3 June 1990 *Tygodnik Powszechny*
published a protest against the anti-democratic propaganda emanating from organisations such as Giertych's and new political parties,
signed by 222 people. Despite the fact that neither *Słowo i Czyn*
nor any of the other groups mentioned in the protest are represented
in the government or, indeed, in parliament, they are widely considered to be a destabilizing factor in the political life of the country.
In May and June 1990 *Tygodnik Powszechny*, the most respected
Catholic paper in Poland, published a number of articles condemning the rise of the nationalistic and anti-semitic right. As a group of
eminent Polish intellectuals stated on 7 May 1990, a new tendency is
emerging – the promotion of the slogan 'Poland for the Poles' and of
the Pole-Catholic stereotype. 'In Polish public life, reference to
Christian values is a natural phenomenon. Such, indeed, is the tradition of "Solidarity". However, cases of utilitarian reference to
Christianity for purposes of political struggle also occur.' A virtually

identical formulation was included in a communique of the Polish Episcopate's Commission for Dialogue with Judaism. Speaking in its name, Monsignor Muszyński expressed anxiety over certain recent anti-semitic manifestations. He reiterated the words of John Paul II: 'Enmity towards, or hatred of, Judaism completely contradicts the Christian vision of human dignity'.[28]

Thus despite the Primate's apparent support for Maciej Giertych, his nationalistic position has been widely criticized, even within the Episcopate.

Throughout June 1989, Jewish organisations attempted to persuade Western Catholics to intercede on their behalf in the Vatican and in Poland. At a ceremony in Sao Paulo, during which he was honoured by the Brazilian Bishops' Conference with the Patriarch Abraham Award for his life-long devotion to strengthening relations between Catholics and Jews, Dr Riegner made an appeal to Cardinal Willebrands, who was similarly honoured, to resolve the serious conflict between the Jewish community and the Polish Church over the convent, which had deeply hurt Jewish feelings and aroused profound emotions.

The government press, such as *Życie Warszawy* (21 June), and *Argumenty* – a militant atheistic weekly – (4 June), reported the objections expressed by various Jewish organizations quoting foreign press agencies, but refraining from any comment. The government was happy to embarrass the Church but at the same time did not want to cause too much damage to Poland's reputation abroad.

A New Site for the Convent

On 5 June 1989, the Archbishop of Lyon, Cardinal Albert Decourtray sent a letter to Theo Klein, in which he announced that the convent would move to a new place – a plot of land some 550 yards further from the camp's perimeter – which would remove all ambiguity about the placement. The new Centre would be separated from the camp by two streets, many buildings and a row of trees. The site, which was approved by the local and regional authorities, belonged to 14 different owners (most of the land still in private hands in Poland is parcelled into tiny plots), and still had to be purchased, although all the owners had promised to sell it to the Archdiocese of Cracow. The Oświęcim Office of Town Planning and Architecture was ready to approve the building plans. This news was greeted by Klein as confirmation that the Church would honour the Geneva Declaration, but other Jewish leaders pointed out that the construction of the new Centre agreed in Switzerland in 1987 would not begin before early 1990. This meant that the extension period of six months requested by Cardinal Decourtray in February 1987, on the second anniversary of the Geneva meeting, and the agreed second deadline for the relocation of the convent would not be kept, as no alternative building to house the nuns before the Centre was finally opened had been made available. This failure to meet the July 1989 deadline for removing the nuns from the convent building was to provoke the most serious protests since the debate began.

On 20 June 1989 Auschwitz was visited by a delegation from the Holocaust Memorial Foundation with its president, Harvey Meyerhoff. The delegation signed an agreement with the Museum in Auschwitz for a long-term loan of 20 years of some of its exhibits to the Museum of the Holocaust in Washington. During the visit, the delegation appealed for mutual restraint. It also suggested a meeting in Washington between the Polish, European, and American Catholic hierarchy, and a number of religious and secular Jewish leaders in order to break the impasse in the dialogue. Such a meeting would, they hoped, lead to a logical and just solution to the problem.[29]

A further expression of Jewish anguish came from Sir Sigmund Sternberg, the Chairman of the International Council of Christians and Jews, in his communication with the then Polish Ambassador in London, Zbigniew Gertych. The Ambassador informed Sternberg that it was a matter for the Church and not for the government to decide.[30]

Communist Government Collapses

In the meantime, however, a major change in Poland's political situation took place. In June 1989, during the first semi-free post-war elections Solidarity was allowed to contest 35 per cent of the seats in the *Sejm* (the Diet, or the lower house of parliament), and all 100 seats in the newly re-established Senate. The result was an absolute victory for the opposition, which won all the seats in the *Sejm* that it was contesting and 99 seats in the Senate, for which the election was totally free. Solidarity was allowed to print its own daily newspaper, *Gazeta Wyborcza*, which played an important part in subsequent discussions about the convent. The election revealed that there had been attempts on the part of the Church hierarchy to support more Catholic nationalistic candidates. Cardinal Glemp received two such Christian Democrats (one of whom was Władysław Siła-Nowicki) a day before the election, making it clear where his sympathies lay. The two official Solidarity candidates Adam Michnik and Jacek Kuroń (both known left-wingers, the former of partially Jewish origin), however, won 66 and 70 percent of the votes respectively.

Divisions within the opposition began to be voiced openly, but the nationalistic line was rejected by the mainstream and the leadership of 'Solidarity'. The organisation has long had close links with the Catholic Church, although its relations with some members of the Church hierarchy, particularly Cardinal Glemp, have been very uneasy.

Polish Criticism of Glemp's Policies

The Cardinal was not one of the more popular bishops. Among the population at large he was respected more for his official, and traditionally very important position as Primate, than for his personal qualities. During the martial law period, he was considered by many Solidarity activists to be far too conciliatory towards the military junta. It was remembered that he had been ready to discipline a number of priests whom the government considered to be too anti-communist by having them removed to remote parishes. It was rumoured at the time, that this banishment was to apply even to Fr Jerzy Popiełuszko, who was to be sent to Rome. Fr Popiełuszko was the best-known priest in Warsaw with an enormous following, not only amongst the workers, but also amongst the intelligentsia. A charismatic preacher, he was a thorn in the authorities' side because of his passionate weekly sermons in which he castigated the government for its abuse of basic human rights, and appealed to the people to uphold moral and ethical values and to live in truth and justice, which he accused the government of failing to do. He was constantly harassed by the secret police and defended by his local bishop, but it was suggested that the Primate was tired of Popiełuszko's confrontations with the authorities. In the end, Popiełuszko was brutally murdered by three officers of the security police before he left for

Rome. The rumours about the Primate's attitude towards this case and his actions against other patriotic priests were strongly resented. Thus, although the Church was closely associated with the political opposition in Poland, and with Solidarity in particular, which used churches as safe meeting-points and refuges for the persecuted, their relationship was complex and depended primarily on the behaviour of particular bishops and local priests. There was a strong Catholic element in Solidarity represented mainly by the lay Catholic liberal intelligentsia. Many meetings of Solidarity supporters were linked to Catholic ceremonies. As one Jewish Solidarity member put it: 'To be in Solidarity meant to participate in meetings under a cross. The cross, however, was widely interpreted as a universal symbol.'[31] Indeed, one of the strange phenomena of the time was the high rate of conversions to the Catholic faith of many adults of Jewish origin. Once again, the old nationalistic notion 'To be a Pole is to be a Catholic' which was rightly criticized as intolerant before the war, resurfaced in a strange and unexpected manner amongst the anticommunist intelligentsia. These were not necessarily nationalistic, but were often left-wing. During the years of martial law and the so-called 'normalisation' which followed, Polish public opinion was highly polarized, but the huge majority totally rejected any kind of compromise with the authorities. As a result support for the Church depended largely on the political stance of its representatives, irrespective of the strength of their religious fervour. During the period of political change, various views and actions on the part of the Church did not gain automatic support. Moreover, it not only became possible, but acceptable openly to criticize various churchmen – something which had previously been avoided so as not to give the Communist government an opportunity to drive a wedge between the people and the Church.

Jewish Support for the Carmelites

In July, the British Board of Jewish Deputies called for a campaign of prayers to be held in British synagogues to show their concern over the convent. A dissenting voice came from Dr Jonathan Webber, a social anthropologist from Oxford and a Fellow in Jewish Social Studies at the Oxford Centre for Postgraduate Hebrew Studies, who had conducted extensive fieldwork in the vicinity of the camp. Dr Webber came out strongly in defence of the nuns because he considered that the convent's building, although it had been used by the Nazis for storage purposes (including cans of Cyklon-B used for gassing the Jews), was never within the camp itself. He considered it unreasonable of the Jews 'to declare that the area clearly *outside* the camp should be set aside for specifically Jewish commemorative purposes; for, if so, how far should our interest extend? Ten yards? 100 yards? The whole of the present city of Oświęcim (Auschwitz)?'.[32] His contribution to the debate raised an interesting point. The Nazis took over a number of buildings in and around the city of Oświęcim, many of which have macabre associations. Oświęcim is now a living town and most of those buildings are used for normal purposes. After the war, the convent itself served for years as a storage place for agricultural produce without arousing any interest on the part of the Jewish community. It is clear that it was the Christian connection with its associated connotations for the Jewish community which had provoked the controversy. Webber applauded the nuns' courage to live 'in the shadow of this appalling place', and to 'face up to the evil head on and on a daily basis'. He suggested that the Jews should do the same instead of attacking the nuns. He asked a rhetorical question:

> How come, in this age of pluralism and multi-cultural reconciliation, that we find it so emotive that members of another faith wish to pray at or near a place that has been hallowed (if that is the right word) by massive Jewish martyrdom?
>
> *Pray!* Who are we, where have we got to nowadays, if we find a group dedicated to prayer and contemplation offensive to us?

Jonathan Webber's letter to the *Jewish Chronicle* provoked a mixed response from its readers. Many angrily disputed his interpretation of the facts. Some considered the convent situated near the place of extermination of so many Jews to be 'an affront to their and our dignity', 'offensive and extremely insensitive to Jewish suffering'. Many pointed out that regardless of the disputed facts, and the moral and ethical questions the crucial factor was that the Church had given an undertaking to move the convent and therefore ought to do so. Both here and throughout the debate in general, some Jewish participants linked the issue of the convent with a variety of others, including the Church's behaviour during the war; the failure of the Vatican to establish diplomatic relations with Israel; the fact that the Pope was Polish and thus not entirely objective by implication; and that he twice received Yasser Arafat in the Vatican. The last criticism shows a lack of understanding of diplomatic and Church procedure. The Pope rarely refuses an audience to an official visitor to the Republic of Italy, regardless of his personal feelings on the subject. There were also, however, some Jewish voices which supported Webber's stance on the issue.

CHAPTER 7

Invasion

Rabbi Weiss Invades the Convent

The conflict about the convent became heated in July 1989 when radical Jewish groups staged new protests at the site. On 14 July, a group of seven Jews wearing striped uniforms as commonly worn during the war in concentration camps, led by Rabbi Avraham Weiss (the head of an orthodox congregation of the Hebrew Institute of Riverdale in New York and a teacher at the local Yeshiva University), climbed over the convent fence and banged on the convent door and windows, demanding that the nuns leave the building. Reports of the incident, which appeared in a great number of Polish and foreign newspapers, varied widely. Rabbi Weiss stated that despite the fact that he came to Poland 'with love and in peace' he and his group were 'ejected from the convent grounds'. The workers building the convents 'pushed us, beat us, threw water over us, insulted us, and tore our clothes'.[1] He therefore felt indignant to be described as the aggressor by the Polish Press Agency. The Solidarity daily, *Gazeta Wyborcza*, gave a full report of the incident on 17 July which included statements from both sides. According to the paper Rabbi Weiss and his group wanted to meet the sisters and explain to them why they should move from the site. The group brought with it placards in Polish, French, English, and Hebrew, demanding that the convent be liquidated at once. After 15 minutes of knocking at the gate with no response, they climbed the fence and found themselves on the convent's courtyard where they began to pray, wearing prayer shawls and blowing horns. The construction workers employed by the convent began to shout at them from the first floor windows, demanding that the group leave the courtyard. One of them drenched the Rabbi with water. After a few hours a group of workers dragged Rabbi Weiss and his followers away in a fairly brutal fashion. The incident was witnessed by a few bystanders who did not intervene and neither did a few policemen who were also

86

present. According to various reports both sides appealed to the police to take action. Rabbi Weiss wanted them to stop the workers from manhandling his group while the workers supposedly decided to eject the trespassers only after repeated appeals to the police to do so failed. The nuns and the Catholic priest who was apparently present did not intervene and were accused by Weiss of turning their backs on the Jews 'just like your Church did 50 years ago'. The Western press described the event as 'one of the worst cases of anti-semitism in Poland since the Communist Party forced thousands of Jews to leave the country in 1968' (*Newsweek* 31 July 1989). Two days later, on 16 July, the same Jewish group demonstrated in Cracow in front of the Marian Cathedral. They were also allowed to enter the courtyard of the Archbishop's Curia where they attached an appeal to Cardinal Macharski to the doors. The text of the appeal was very restrained:

> Dear Cardinal Macharski, we come in peace, but at the same time we are afraid. We come to appeal for justice for our dead who cannot speak for themselves. ... As proud Jews we announce – stop praying for the Jews who were killed in the *Shoah*, let them rest in peace as Jews.

In a conversation with a representative of the Curia the group stated that they were not interested in any dialogue as long as the convent remained in place because the Catholic Church wanted to 'remove the Jewish character of the *Shoah* and give it a Christian character'. As Reuters reported, the group handed a letter to the Catholic authorities which stated that Cardinal Macharski should resign if the convent was not removed and if he did not punish the nuns for 'watching in silence as workers beat Jews'.[2]

Later the same day, Rabbi Weiss and his followers, after again climbing over the convent fence, staged a six-hour long demonstration during which they sang religious songs and displayed banners saying 'Leave our dead alone', and 'Remove the convent'. The onlookers gathered on the other side of the street did not intervene and the sisters refused to leave the convent and call the police (who did not intervene either). The group climbed back over the fence and left peacefully. Both events roused the interest of many local inhabitants and some visitors, including Jewish ones who refused, however, to participate in Rabbi Weiss's actions. It also attracted enormous interest on the part of the press.

The Polish Episcopate Reproaches Weiss

The first incident attracted the attention of the Metropolitan Curia of Cracow which issued a communique on 15 July signed by the Vice-Chancellor of the Curia, Fr Jan Dyduch, describing the incident and commenting that the local population was outraged by the behaviour of the protesters who 'hurled abuse at the sisters, Poles, and the Church. Workers and passers-by drew attention to their improper behaviour and demanded that they leave immediately. Various forms of persuasion and discussion continued until 5 pm when the intruders were moved outside the gate'.

Two days later, the Curia issued another communique criticizing the behaviour of Rabbi Weiss and pointing out that it was an unlawful disturbance of the peace and 'incommodated the sisters in their prayers and normal daily business'. The Chancellor of the Curia, Fr Bronisław Fidelus, also criticized the second demonstration by the same group, pointing out that July 16 was the feast of Our Lady of the Scapular during which the relatives of the sisters had a right to visit the nuns, and other Carmelite nuns were unable to enter the convent because of the Jewish demonstration. In saying so he referred to the fact that the Discalced Carmelites were an enclosed order with a strict rule which prohibited contact with the outside world – even their relatives had restricted access. Fr Fidelus also demanded, (though this was not part of the official statement), that these incidents should cease because the American Jews who participated in it had been guilty of trespass, even though they were the 'representatives of a society which voices and maintains the principle that the property of others is sacred'.

On 18 July, the Polish Episcopate's Commission for Dialogue with Judaism issued a statement expressing the view that the behaviour of Rabbi Weiss and his group constituted violation of the law which 'could not possibly contribute to the resolution of the conflict', and appealed for better mutual comprehension by way of dialogue and mutual respect. At the same time, the Commission restated that 'the implementation of these decisions [from Geneva] must not be allowed to be delayed by any misunderstandings or incidents' and declared that it fully shared the position of the Jewish organisations in Poland on the issue.

The communiques were published in *Tygodnik Powszechny* on 30 July, together with a statement from Jewish organizations and the Chief Rabbi of Poland in which they expressed their concern about the incidents and described them as contrary to Jewish religious law and to the moral and ethical principles of Judaism. They accepted that conditions were still propitious for the realization of the Geneva agreement.

Public Debate Continues

A large number of articles describing the incidents appeared both in Poland and abroad. Some were inflammatory and some conciliatory. The official Solidarity daily, *Gazeta Wyborcza*, published an article written by one of the editors, a leading Catholic layman, and currently the Polish ambassador to Morocco, Krzysztof Śliwiński.[3] In it he regretted that the agreement made in Geneva had not yet been implemented and stated that the conflict would not be resolved as long as the Poles did not make attempts to look at the problems through the eyes of the Jews. At the same time, he was pained by the attitude of those Jews who demonstrated on the site who thought that 'the ends justified the means'. 'All provocative gestures, even in the interests of peace, have two sides. They arouse the interest of the public but at the same time create a climate which is not conducive to solving the conflict.' Śliwiński's main object of attack was, however, the behaviour of the Polish participants in the incident, which he thought indicated an outrageous and deep-seated intolerance. He considered their actions disproportionately brutal. He also criticized the police and the clergy for not intervening which he said was impossible to justify.

On 18 July, *Gazeta Wyborcza* published interviews with Rabbi Weiss and Jacek Kuroń, presently a Minister in the Solidarity-led Government, responsible for ethnic minorities, as well as statements from Bishop Muszyński and Fr Musiał, Secretary of the Commission of the Polish Episcopate for Dialogue with Judaism. Jacek Kuroń assured the Jews that he felt deeply ashamed as a Pole about what had happened. Monsignor Muszyński stated that 'the feelings of the Jews towards this place are very different. This has become increasingly clear to us. The feelings of the Poles are different. It seems to me that we ought to respect this diversity.' Fr Musiał attempted to explain that there are religious differences between Jews and Christians, particularly in the way they regard their own dead. Jews do not like to disturb their peace. On the other hand, he said, if one has something to discuss, one should not enter via the fence. In a letter from the Episcopal Press Office, Fr Musiał stressed that considering that the overwhelming majority of the camp's victims were Jewish, one should not be 'surprised that Auschwitz has become a symbol of the Holocaust, although it is also a symbol of martyrdom for the Polish nation and although people of 26 nationalities from 26 countries died here. The symbols are sacred and unquestionable. If we want Auschwitz to be recognised as a symbol of martyrdom of the Polish people in such a sense as we most deeply feel it, we must take all the pains to try to sense how another nation or nations understand and experience Auschwitz as a symbol of their martyrdom'.

Another interview with Weiss was published in the daily *Życie Warszawy* of 18 July. In it Weiss claimed that it was sacrilege towards those who died to have a Catholic convent in this particular place. They died as Jews, therefore they should be honoured in their own faith. The presence of the Carmel violated their peace. At the same time, Weiss was against the establishment of the ecumenical Centre agreed in Geneva.

On the 20 July a delegation of the World Jewish Congress which included Rabbi Marvin Hier of the Simon Wiesenthal Centre, went to the Vatican to ask the Pope to intervene in the conflict. The delegation was received by Monsignor Luigi Gatti from the Secretariat of State, and by Monsignor Gerard Daucourt from the Office for Relations with Judaism. The delegation was informed that the Pope had decided not to become engaged in the controversy and left it entirely to the Polish Church. This displeased Rabbi Hier who said that it was very depressing that the only person who could have solved the problem did not want to become involved in it.[4]

On 21 July, information boards displaying architectural designs for the future Ecumenical Centre were put up. This was the first time the Polish public learned about the plans for the convent in any detail. The Centre was to consist of two buildings containing exhibition and conference halls, a library, and a pilgrims' hostel. The new cloister was to be built on the premises and separated from the outside by a wall. The Centre would occupy approximately four hectares (10 acres). This announcement came as a late assurance to the local population that the nuns would not be completely dispossessed.

Demonstrations at Auschwitz

As Reuters reported, a group of 300 Jews intended to demonstrate on 23 July in front of the convent. Reuters was criticized in the Polish press for deliberate sensationalism after they described the incident with Rabbi Weiss as 'one of the most revolting scenes of violence against the Jews to take place in Poland for many years.'

A large group of local onlookers gathered by the convent on the day of the demonstration, largely out of curiosity, but also fearing that this rather large Jewish group would attempt to repeat the performance of Rabbi Weiss. In the end, only about 100 Jews representing the Belgian Students Union and the World Jewish Congress turned up. The demonstrators carried banners in Polish and French saying 'Do not Christianize Auschwitz and *Shoah*!'. They blew a *shofar* [ram's horn ritual trumpet] as in Jericho, trying to 'symbolically bring down the walls of hate separating Gentile and Jew'. They also read statements in English and French, but ironically not in Polish, thus making little attempt to bring down the above-mentioned walls. There was also a French group lead by the Chief Rabbi of France, Samuel Sirat, who prayed in front of the convent. As the Rabbi stated, they were not protesting against the convent, but demanding that this site should remain a memorial in the spirit of the Geneva agreement. As he subsequently wrote: 'No one in the world has the right to transform into a place of prayer this place where the most appalling idolatry was practiced, by man proclaiming the death of God and striving to make himself divine by reducing other human creatures to the condition of objects, non-persons. Such prayers risk becoming, according to the biblical expression, "an abomination". Auschwitz must absolutely become a place of absolute silence, non-prayer, non-testimony, evidence of paroxysm and havoc ... Let us all, together, make ours the words of the psalmist, "For you, Lord, the silence alone is prayer".'[5]

Local Inhabitants Express Their Hostility

The local inhabitants who waited for a long time for the demonstration to materialize, expressed a variety of opinions, largely hostile to the Jews. These were reported in Polish and emigre publications. It was felt that the Western Jews had done nothing for their brethren during the War when the nuns sheltered Jewish children. American Jewry was particularly criticized for its pushiness, in contrast to the War when they had remained passive. The Israeli treatment of the Palestinians and of the intifada was contrasted with the peace-loving image which the Jews wanted to project in Poland.

The respected monthly *Kultura*, the doyen of emigre publications, devoted much space to the controversy. Tomasz Jerz (a pseudonym), published an eye-witness report of the demonstration, recording comments made by the onlookers before the demonstration began:

> "We live in a free Poland," shouts some female. "The Jews should stay at home. Get back to Palestine! We are defending our ⟨ ⟩. We won't let anyone take the convent."
> "If you went to their country and entered a synagogue without a hat and carried on the way they do here they'd kill you on the spot, no questions asked."
> "The Sisters pray for everyone the Germans killed in the camps. For the scabs too. What are they after here?"
> "That television crew is probably Jewish too. Why don't they show what they do at home? They murder just like Hitler, they're fighting a war."
> "They crucified our God, they killed Jesus," a young boy with a possessed look shouted hysterically. "They killed Jesus, the priest said so in church."
> "Poland is a rich country," shrieked another woman. "We have everything: land, sea. Foreigners have ruined us, those damned Jews. They come here, buy everything in the shops, there's nothing left because of them. I want to eat Polish meat, not some Arab stuff."

The inhabitants of Oświęcim were portrayed as anti-Jewish, although the individual singled out for his anti-semitism was a member of the Roman Dmowski society who distributed leaflets accusing Solidarity leaders, including Prime Minister Mazowiecki, of being Jewish, and the much-respected senator and co-founder in the 1970s of the Workers' Self-Defence Committee KOR, Jan Józef Lipski, of being a socialist representing German interests in Poland. Ironically, he was chased away by the crowd.

As Jerz commented, the crowd was full of hatred, but its outbursts were random and indiscriminate, despite the fact that on this occasion it had gathered because of the Jews. The crowd was poor, ugly, and wretched. For years they had been subjected to a daily grind which brought nothing but poverty and deprivation. They resented the fact that no attempt was made to communicate with them and considered the events to have been staged largely for the benefit of the foreign media. This view was echoed by the Polish press. They also saw the Jews as insincere because they allowed synagogues and Jewish cemeteries in Poland to go to ruin, but had no qualms about interfering in Polish Church affairs.

However, there were also views supportive of the Jewish position:

> "I know this is our country and no foreigner will lord over us, but if these Jews feel so strongly about this particular place, can't we be more considerate and find another place for the convent?"

> "I can understand these Jews. Cardinal Macharski has apparently pledged to remove the convent. So let him keep his promise."

Dr Jerzy Gitter, a professor emeritus of Boston University, a Polish Jew who was amongst the crowd said:

> "I don't find this cross offensive at all, and this land is only symbolically Jewish. The place is Church property, after all, and in America you are free to top your house with anything you like, the cross, the Star of David, whatever. The convent is outside the camp compound and I, for one, wouldn't demonstrate for its closure. But these young Jews want a demo here and I believe they have every right to stage it and speak their minds. It's democracy, you see."[6]

In the end, the demonstration was much smaller than expected, dignified, and entirely peaceful, despite the tension apparent beforehand.

Weiss Attracts World-wide Attention

On 24 July *Gazeta Wyborcza* published a number of letters from Polish and Jewish readers. Fr Dominik Wider, Father General of the Discalced Carmelites in Poland, criticized the Geneva agreements for demanding unilateral concessions from the Catholics and accused the Jewish side of intolerable behaviour bordering on blackmail. He described the intrusion of Rabbi Weiss as a raid, involving trespass, verbal abuse of the sisters, attempts to break in and the virtual imprisonment of the sisters and their guests for many hours. He denied that there was a cleric amongst the workers or that anybody was drenched with water. He denounced the dialogue with the Jews because, as he said, all of them ended with a Jewish monologue, 'No arguments reach them. Their arguments are groundless.' He ended by objecting to the principle of relocating the nuns and pointed out that they had in any case nowhere to go as no alternative building had been prepared. Two other letters condemned the incident as immoral and criminal and described Rabbi Weiss as a fanatic and appealed for him to apologize to the nuns, or for his arrest. Stanisław Krajewski, a well-known Polish Jew, tried to explain in his letter why Auschwitz was a symbol of the Jewish Holocaust and regretted that the Geneva agreement had not been implemented. He pointed out that the Jews did not object to Catholic prayer on the site as such, but rather to 'institutionalized prayer'. While sympathetic to the position of the Polish Episcopate, he felt that it was not entirely credible because it did not specify the exact date on which the convent would be moved.

On 29 July, the party weekly *Polityka* published an article describing the various stages of the conflict and the position of both sides. The main part of the article dealt with the incursion of Rabbi Weiss and Polish reactions to it, saying that disagreements were more to do with interpretation and the intentions of the participants than with the facts. The article quoted Rabbi Weiss, who justified his behaviour on three grounds: first, he stated that the UNESCO World Heritage Convention stipulated that certain sites were inviolable and that the convent was precisely on one of those sites. Therefore he and his group were not trespassing when they climbed over the fence, since the ground did not belong to the Church but to mankind. Secondly, Cardinal Macharski had not kept the Geneva agreement; thirdly, Auschwitz was for him a symbol of the murder of Jews simply because they were Jewish. His behaviour was therefore the result, rather than the cause of the problems. On another occasion Rabbi Weiss justified his actions by stating that he only wanted to talk to the nuns and to present his case to them directly. According to this report the nuns made an attempt to talk to Rabbi Weiss after his second intrusion on 16 July, but he intimated to them through a chance translator that there could be no dialogue as long as the nuns remained there.

The article quoted a local police officer, Zbigniew Kaczmarczyk, who admitted that he had received a request for help from the nuns on 14 July, but had refused to escort the demonstrators out of the convent without first receiving a formal request in writing. This may have been the result of a general demoralisation of the police force which was widespread in Poland at the time. The police had for decades been closely associated with the Communist regime in peoples's eyes and, after Solidarity's victory in the first semi-free elections, were uneasy about their position. To have been seen intervening in the convent dispute could have been misinterpreted by the local population as acting against the nuns, and this could have resulted in serious problems for the police. It is also likely that the police were reluctant to become involved in a controversy involving both the Church and the foreign media. The Church's difficulties were, in any case, unlikely to have caused the police force much worry. Unofficial police intervention by a plain-clothes officer apparently took place anyway when the construction workers were reprimanded at their first attempt to evict the demonstrators. The workers themselves blamed the police by saying: 'How is it that when we tried to do something the first time they stopped us, and the second time they turned a blind eye?' The workers explained that their involvement was a result of police non-intervention. Captain Kaczmarczyk (the head of the regional Security Service – the notorious political branch of the police), claimed that most of the protestors came from Belgium, and also from America, but that Israelis did not take part in these demonstrations.

The Mother Superior of the convent was quoted as saying that pouring water over Weiss was regrettable and was a stupid practical joke on the part of one of the workers who was mentally retarded. The same article in *Polityka* printed a comment by Minister Lorenz, Communist Minister for Religious Affairs, who said that the Communist government disclaimed all responsibility for the matter since it was not party to the Geneva agreement. He stated, however, that the agreed period for implemention of two years struck him as too short, taking into account Polish conditions, and that although the agreement was still valid and binding, it would be better to return to the spirit of the agreement instead of demonstrating. The official government organ *Rzeczpospolita* of 25 July expressed its concern about the July incident and its international repercussions.

There were numerous reactions in the foreign press to the events in Poland. Neil Ascherson, in his article 'One More Horror at Auschwitz' in the *Observer*, considered that it was 'hard to imagine a more desolating and unnecessary row. On the one hand is the enduring tactlessness of elements in the Catholic church, especially in Poland, towards Jewish feelings. On the other is Jewish neo-zealotry, almost entirely American, spoiling for a fight with real or imagined anti-semites anywhere on earth – as long as the TV cameras are there.' As he pointed out, the events can be evaluated in two different ways. The ejection of Rabbi Weiss could be regarded as a 'brutal but predictable response to male raiders breaking into a nunnery', but it could also be seen as 'a minor anti-semitic atrocity. Elan Steinberg, executive director of the World Jewish Congress in New York, declared: "Part of Auschwitz has become *Judenrein* (the Nazi term for Jew-free)!"'.

Ascherson despaired that Auschwitz was being fought over like the Holy Places in Israel. He considered Cardinal Macharski's view that the Carmel was 'the living monument of crimes of expiation for crimes done by men in the past' to be a more admirable response than the attitudes of some Jews that the Polish Pope was a Jew-hater and that the Church's failure to remove the convent was as bad as the Vatican's failure to denounce the Holocaust itself.[7]

Peter Simple in the *Daily Telegraph* was far less charitable, 'Some of the utterances of these Jewish activists are terrifying in their fanaticism and unappeasable thirst for vengeance. The protests against the nuns will continue until they are driven out, says Mr Eli Steinberg of the World Jewish Congress in New York ... these Jewish fanatics, at their most extreme, seem almost to have persuaded themselves that Jews were the only people who were massacred in the Second World War. "Auschwitz" they seem to be saying, "is ours and ours alone for ever."' On another occasion, he found Cardinal Glemp guilty primarily of 'pro-Polonism. He is speaking on behalf of his own Polish people, who, because of the fanatical and arrogant behaviour of the Jewish activists at Auschwitz, must now be more than ever united in their determination that the nuns shall remain there. So to the original contention, surely acceptable to non-fanatical people whether Jew or Gentile, that the nuns should remain in this accursed place because they are praying for all its victims, has been added a new argument, specifically Catholic and Polish, reinforcing in its turn the fanaticism of the Jewish activists and making them more than ever determined to claim Auschwitz for their people alone.'[8]

Chaim Bermant in the *Jewish Chronicle* considered the use of force not conducive in the advancement of moral arguments. He described the action of Rabbi Weiss as an unjustified escapade and criticized the World Jewish Congress for calling the Polish workers' reaction a 'vicious and unprovoked attack'. As Bermant stated 'To read some American reports of their foray, one would think that Weiss and company were the innocent victims of a pogrom. Weiss, who may have been a double-glazing salesman in an earlier incarnation, explains that he merely wanted to talk to the nuns, but they didn't want to be talked to – as was their right – nor did they welcome his intrusion.' Bermant called Weiss's behaviour 'an exercise in false heroics' which 'may have undone the patient efforts of many men over many years. But he has received no word of reproof from any established authority.' He goes on to accuse the American Jews of having a bad conscience because they did not do enough to stave off the Holocaust when it was taking place and were now attempting to appease their conscience by over-reacting. He concedes that there was little more American Jewry could have done, nevertheless, 'one cannot redress the impotence of one age with excessive zeal in another'.[9]

Bermant's position was subsequently supported by some readers of the *Jewish Chronicle* who considered Rabbi Weiss's action primitive and highly provocative, closing the door to understanding and strengthening the 'barriers from which xenophobia and its derivative, anti-semitism, spring'. Dr Shenkin, writing from Glasgow, continued by denouncing the 'self-assured feelings of justification' of Jewish students and ridiculed their claim that the refusal to allow them entry into the convent constituted their 'Jewish spirituality being denied'. He asked 'Is it not understandable that Polish workmen, witnessing the same attempt to enter, would react as if harmless nuns were being threatened? Could it be that two small, self-selected xenophobic groups felt threatened by each other?'[10] This view was shared by some readers, but not all. One remarked that he understood the motives of Rabbi Weiss and considered Chaim Bermant misguided for 'applying English standards of tolerance to Polish society in which he has never lived'.[11]

Jewish Preconceptions

Over the next month, Bermant came under strong attack from other Jews. Typical was a letter completely misrepresenting the Catholic view of the Holocaust; 'seemingly, the Carmelite order, as do some other segments of the Roman Catholic church, regard the Holocaust as divine punishment on the Jews for their rejection of Jesus.' The author continued in the same erroneous vein, first by stating that the convent was a memorial to Edith Stein 'whose death was in expiation of the "sin" of the Jews who had perished in the camp', and secondly it suggested that the Catholics considered her martyrdom to be 'a posthumous "redemption" ... for those who died there.'[12] This ignored the fact that the nuns abandoned their original plan to dedicate the convent to Edith Stein as soon as they realised the offence it would cause to some Jews. In general, the letter displayed ignorance of the teaching of the Church on the Jews after the Second Vatican Council.

Another regular fallacy was that the Carmelites were attempting to baptise murdered Jews. From a Catholic doctrinal point of view this is absurd. The author's angry reaction to Christian proselytism was made apparent by her reference to 'smug missionaries' on Jewish doorsteps.[13]

A strongly-worded response to Chaim Bermant and Dr Shenkin came from Mike Sarne of London who claimed that Bermant 'knows full well that these meditative madonnas are earnestly employed in white-washing bloodstains for the Church of Rome. They are in the vanguard of turning the black hell where a Roman Catholic monster many times worse than Torquemada, murdered his Jewish prey, into a pretty market garden where saintly spinsters do a bit of meditating.'

Referring to the event much later in *Le Monde* of 29 August, Emile Malet, editor of *Passages*, and Daniel Lindenberg of the editorial board of *L'Esprit* called Rabbi Weiss and his group 'American Jewish commandos who insulted the Carmelites and who bear a heavy responsibility for it'. Barbara Amiel, writing for the *Times*, complained about the small-mindedness of the American protesters. She did not think Auschwitz, a place where millions of Jews were murdered, was necessarily the best site for a convent, but the decision to locate it there seemed 'dwarfed by the awesome stupidity of American rabbis in striped pyjamas trying, in a Catholic country to prevent nuns from praying – *praying*, for heaven's sake – to the same God.' She considered that issuing resolutions to evict the nuns and marching in front of the convent showed 'a lack of taste, humility, and wisdom that is quite astonishing'.[15]

The American demonstrators were also condemned by Itshak Levy, a representative of the National Religious Party in the Knesset (Israeli Parliament). After his official visit to the death camps he said 'It was annoying to see that American Jews were more involved in the convent issue than the State of Israel. American Jews know how to criticise, but they are sitting in the US and not coming to Israel. They should leave the matter to Israeli diplomacy – Israel is the official representative of the Jewish people – instead of doing damage to the cause.' Another Knesset member who was not part of the mission, Rabbi Avraham Verdiger from the orthodox Agudat Israel Party disagreed, saying that all Jews have the right to protest against the convent's 'monopolisation of the death camp'.[16]

The Convent's Location Disputed

On 30 July, *Tygodnik Polski* a weekly of the Christian Social Union – a vaguely pro-Communist Christian organisation – published a long account of the conflict quoting Jewish and Catholic officials extensively and expressing surprise that the Jewish side maintained that the convent was situated on the site of the former camp. The article quoted a letter of March 1986 from Kazimierz Smoleń, director of the Auschwitz-Birkenau museum and an ex-inmate of Auschwitz, to Lucjan Motyka, Secretary General of the International Auschwitz Committee, in which he stated that the convent building was outside the borders of the Auschwitz camp and separated from it by a concrete wall. He said that the building, originally intended to be a theatre, was used throughout the war as a small warehouse for household goods. 'The question of whether Cyklon B gas might have been occasionally stored in its cellars is purely a matter of speculation.' The article criticizes the decision of the International Auschwitz Committee of 28–29 April 1989, which stated that the building housing the convent was 'an integral part of the Auschwitz State Museum', as being contrary to Smoleń's statement and the facts. The article also quotes the protests of local Catholics against the decision of the Church authorities to relocate the convent and claimed that there had been a number of attempts throughout 1986–88 by Jewish pilgrims to invade the convent, involving verbal abuse and aggressive threats towards the nuns. The paper was clearly attempting to turn Catholic opinion against the Church hierarchy when it quoted a letter of 18 January 1989 from the Provincial of the Discalced Carmelites in Poland addressed to all members of the order. (The letter was published a few months later by the pro-Communist Catholic daily *Słowo Powszechne*, having been refused publication by recognized Catholic papers.) In his letter, Fr Dominik stated 'For some time there has been an increase in malicious Jewish attacks and of moral pressure from Cardinal Macharski on our sisters in Auschwitz to voluntarily agree to be relocated. Arguments used include love of one's neighbour, not obstructing the dialogue between the Church and the Jews, not providing grounds for attacking the Holy Father and the Church in Poland ... I have lodged a protest with Cardinal Macharski and also with a non-Polish representative of the Church, Cardinal Lustiger. I have also appealed to our Father General. I wish to inform you that almost all the bishops of the Krakow diocese are outraged by this pressure exerted on the sisters. The clergy of Oświęcim and its vicinities and many of the faithful share their indignation.'

The paper describes the attitude of Jewish leaders in the West as uncompromising and emotional. It then attacks the French Cardinals for relying entirely on information provided by the Jews which the article attributes to the recent history of France, implying that the French were compensating for their anti-semitism during the war. The article ends with a statement made in *Tygodnik Powszechny* (22 June 1989) by its editor, Jerzy Turowicz, in which he explains that the Jews are afraid that the symbolism of Auschwitz will be appropriated by the Poles and will cease to be a symbol of Jewish *Shoah*.

Jewish Exclusivity

Turowicz disagrees with this view, pointing out that there is no danger of such a reinterpretation of history occuring in Poland, as opposed to in France where there are people (like Faurisson) denying that the Holocaust had ever taken place. He appeals to the public to treat everything related to the tragic fate of the Jews with respect, even if the Jews show some over-sensitivity. However, while acknowledging the Jewish right to regard Auschwitz as a symbol of the *Shoah*, Turowicz does not grant them an exclusive right to the camp: 'The Jews should know and understand the importance of Auschwitz in the collective consciousness of our nation.' Here Turowicz reminds readers of the several hundred thousand Polish victims, representing the best elements of Polish society, who also died in Auschwitz.

The view of Jewish exclusivity was shared even by those interested in Christian-Jewish dialogue. In a little-known report from the first meeting in Geneva in July 1986 Professor Ady Steg, President of the *Alliance Israélite Universelle*, proclaimed that there were hundreds of thousands of non-Jews murdered in Auschwitz and that their memory 'deserves to be preserved in piety', but 'their murder was perpetrated as an "extra measure" ... a matter of subjecting the non-Jews to facilities which were installed for the working out of the Final Solution. In truth, Auschwitz, with its gas chambers and its crematoria, was conceived, constructed and put to use solely for the extermination of the Jews.'

Father John T. Pawlikowski OSM, a theologian much involved in Christian-Jewish dialogue, criticized this statement as an extreme example of lack of historical knowledge on the part of the Jews. According to him, this problem applied partially also to some prominent Western Catholics, including Cardinal Lustiger.[17]

On some of these points the views of Turowicz did not differ from those of a French Jewish historian, Pierre Vidal-Naquet, who emphasised that there was never any question of any Pole doubting that the Holocaust did take place, or denying the existence of the gas chambers. In an interview published in *Regards* he stated that it was inappropriate to talk about such Polish revisionism with regard to Auschwitz. This stands in stark contrast to an Israeli historian (a disciple of Faurisson) who did publish an article in Hebrew, in an Israeli journal, claiming that the gas chambers did not exist.[18]

Various opinions were expressed on the issue throughout the period. *Polityka* of 5 August 1989 published a letter from Samuel Dombrowski from Dusseldorf, a Jew who survived the war in Poland and whose entire family perished in Auschwitz, in which he said that he was grateful for the prayers of the Carmelites, comparing them to the prayers and actions of Bishop von Gallen and Pastor Bonhoeffer during the war, and expressed his hopes that the dialogue between the Jews and the Church would continue. He also reminded readers that convents had often been the last refuge for persecuted Jews, especially children, who were hidden by the nuns, regardless of the dangers involved. He pointed out that the cross which aroused so much passion signified, during the war, a place of rescue and safety for those hunted and desperately trying to survive.

Indeed, despite the Church's very mixed record in its treatment of the Jews during the War, that of various convents was remarkable. The precise number of Jews saved by religious orders in Poland is unknown, but it is thought to be several thousand children and a few hundred adults. A Jewish survivor and historian, Szymon Datner has said, in respect of the female religious orders: 'In my research I have found only one case of help being refused. No other sector was so ready to help those persecuted by the Germans, including the Jews;

this attitude, unanimous and general, deserves recognition and respect.'[19] Despite the presence of many blackmailers and denouncers, there is no known case in Poland of anybody sheltered in a convent falling victim to their activities.

The student weekly (Communist controlled) *Itd* of 6 August 1989 published an article by Alina Ert-Eberdt questioning Jewish attempts to establish exclusive rights over the camp. The author saw nothing unusual in the fact that the Carmelites, an enclosed order devoted to prayer and meditation, wanted to establish a small community devoted to the commemoration of the victims of the camp, similar to the German Carmelites who had previously established a cloister at Dachau. The building chosen was a derelict storage house without water, sanitation or heating which had been abandoned for years. The Oświęcim town council had given it to the nuns on a long term lease (99 years). The article considered Jewish protests to be based on a misunderstanding, since the protestors claimed that Jews were the only victims and failed to realize that the camp was a symbol of all concentration camps.

Ert-Eberdt tried to explain that the huge cross, which caused additional problems when it was put up by the convent, was the one used on the altar in Birkenau during the Pope's visit there in 1979, and that it was now placed on the gravel where Germans used to shoot the first Polish prisoners of Auschwitz before the so-called Wall of Death was built.

The article gives an overview of the debate so far and stresses the distinction between Auschwitz where there were substantial Polish losses, and Birkenau (Auschwitz II). She questions the validity of creating national enclaves within Auschwitz I. The author goes on to quote Jewish voices sympathetic to the Carmelites, such as Rabbi Zalman Schechter from Philadelphia, and claims that the Mother Superior of the convent had, as a young girl, smuggled food to the ghetto. The article concludes that the camp is a symbol for all humanity and as such should not divide. The mention of the Mother Superior's involvement with the Jews during the War was accurate. As a child she was asked by her mother to take food to the Jews since she was less conspicuous than an adult. She was probably not fully aware of the nature of this activity nor of the automatic death penalty which applied to those caught. But of course this made the entire row about the convent even more paradoxical.

In early August 1989, press agencies reported Rabbi Abraham Weiss's announcement that he was going to sue the workers who had ejected him from the convent and the policemen who did not intervene. He also demanded that Israel should take over the administration of the Auschwitz-Birkenau complex as a symbol of the destruction of the Jews. 'If Israel does not administer and supervise Auschwitz it will be impossible to preserve the unique message of this place where the Nazis attempted to liquidate the Jews.'

CHAPTER 8

Agreement Suspended

Macharski Suspends Implementation of the Geneva Agreement

On 8th August 1989 Cardinal Macharski issued a statement which was subsequently published in various newspapers. The statement came as a response to numerous queries about his views on the anti-Carmel campaign. In it, the Cardinal bowed to pressure, announcing:

> The delay in meeting the unrealistic deadline for the completion of the Centre has caused a violent campaign of accusations and slander by some Jewish groups in the West; of abusive aggression, not only verbal, which was taken into Oświęcim itself. No respect was shown for the Sisters' human and Christian dignity, destroying the peace which was their right. They failed to respect Christian beliefs and the symbols of faith and piety. The desires and intentions of the Church were presented and interpreted in a one-sided manner and hostile intentions attributed to them. As regards the intrusion on the convent grounds and rampaging through it, I heard only one voice calling for restraint – the voice of Jewish organisations in Poland.

This kind of attitude and action made it impossible for him to continue work on building the centre.

> In this atmosphere of aggressive demands and unrest to which we have been subjected, there is no way of showing a common concern for the building of a place of mutual respect, without abandoning one's own religious and national beliefs. The desire for peace must lie at the foundations of a work of peace. I desire peace and I will not violate it. If it should be necessary, I remind my community of the need to retain dignity and self-control in word and deed. I regret that this has not been understood by the responsible people of some Jewish organisations.

This unexpected statement by a signatory of the Geneva agreement caused a new storm of protests from the Jewish organisations and was a source of anxiety for some Polish Catholics and for the foreign signatories of the Geneva accords.

On 11 August, Cardinal Decourtray issued a short communique distancing himself from Cardinal Macharski by saying that the decision taken in Geneva 'will not be questioned ... Demonstrations and deplorable reactions can have no influence on the issue discussed by the agreement of 22 February.'

Monsignor Alberto Ablondi, the head of the Italian Bishops' Conference for Dialogue with Protestants, Orthodox, and Jews, stated that the Church had a duty to honour its commitment. Referring to Rabbi Weiss's actions the Bishop spoke about the 'grave intemperances' and requested moderation on the part of the Jews. At the same time, he showed great understanding of Jewish sensitivities about the issue and stated that the convent in Auschwitz 'could be an offering at the altar of the common faith in God on the part of the Christians, but if this offering offends the Jewish brother, it is our duty to renounce it and to give precedence to reconciliation.'[1]

The publication of Cardinal Macharski's statement coincided with a long article by an eminent lay Catholic, Professor Jacek Woźniakowski, published in *Tygodnik Powszechny* on 13 August, in which he attempted to explain the philosophical and religious issues behind the controversy. Although he expressed surprise that it was this particular convent which had aroused so much Jewish indignation, considering that the Parish Church of the Blessed Virgin Mary Queen of Poland had existed since 1983 in the building that had housed the Nazi administration of Birkenau (the part of the camp complex where most Jews were murdered) and had not attracted any attention, he nevertheless strongly urged the nuns to move. He considered the convent, although outside the camp's perimeter, to be an 'integral part of the camp's horrific past'. He considered it paradoxical that the very people who objected to the silent prayer of the Carmelites as disturbing the peace of the camp, were the same people who were creating uproar in the place itself. For Woźniakowski, 'a concentration camp is a most inappropriate place for silly, stupid, or vulgar actions, for Polish, anti-Polish, or any other propaganda'. He considered that 'the noisy invasion of the grounds of a convent can lead to nothing good'. He admitted that, had he been one of the workers present, and if peaceful persuasion had failed to bring results, he would probably have helped to remove the intruders, regardless of who they might have been. The intruders had come to the convent with a group of photographers for the specific purpose of having their action widely reported, fully prepared for the fact that they might be forcibly removed and manhandled which, in publicity terms, would further their cause.

Woźniakowski characterized the negative features of the mass media as noisiness, jumping to conclusions, hysteria, and gossip-mongery. At the same time, he stressed that its positive characteristics far outweighed these faults. The Catholic Church, according to him, had not proved itself well able to adapt to the style of the modern media. In a veiled criticism of Cardinal Macharski's *modus operandi*, he described the typically traditional reaction of the Church 'in which there is a very fine dividing line between caution and procrastination, discretion and concealment, a slow search for compromise and temporization'.

It was essential, Woźniakowski insisted, that the Geneva agreement should be implemented as soon as possible regardless of objective difficulties and that every move in this direction should be publicised. During this period the Jewish organisations which had demonstrated in Auschwitz should refrain from enflaming passions and exerting pressure. He ended by stating that it was scandalous that the blood of millions should be the object of petty conflict.

On the same day, *Tygodnik Demokratyczny* [Democratic Weekly] which was the official organ of *Stronnictwo Demokratyczne* [Democratic Party], until 1989 a pseudo-independent pro-communist party, published an article describing the background of events and appealing for calm. The article contained two important pronouncements made by Jewish leaders – by Theodore Freedman, European Director of the Anti-Defamation League, B'nai B'rith, and Gerard Breibart, of the Jewish Central Council in West Germany. Freedman stated that there was nothing sinister about the Carmelite nuns' motives for establishing a convent in Auschwitz and that their presence did not diminish the tragedy of the Jewish nation which took place there. Breibart, appearing on German television, claimed that there was nothing wrong with the establishment of the convent for purposes of expiation, providing Jewish religious law was observed, that is to say that a church should not be built where the Jews are buried. He thought that 'the symbol of praying and expiating nuns in Oświęcim would certainly be understood by the Jews and accepted by them.' He remarked, however, that he 'was not speaking in the name of all the Jews.' However, these remarks were made before Cardinal Macharski's decision to postpone the implementation of the agreement.

Jews Shocked at Macharski's Abrogation

The World Jewish Congress considered Cardinal Macharski's statement to be 'a tragic blow for all those members of the Jewish and Catholic communities who have worked for so long to create mutual understanding and respect.' The Congress appealed to the Vatican to overrule Cardinal Macharski's decision, adding that silence from the Vatican on this issue would be 'the repetition of a historic tragedy'.[2] The President of the European Division of B'nai B'rith, Lutz Ehrlich, said that Cardinal Macharski's statement was 'an absolutely unacceptable act of breaking the agreement'.[3]

In the meantime, the controversy was further complicated by one of the Pope's homilies at his weekly audience in St Peter's Square, which was taken to imply that God had made a new covenant with the Christians because the Jews had failed to live according to divine law. This caused uproar in Israel, Western Europe, and in the United States. In England a leading London Rabbi, Jeffrey Cohen, considered it 'particularly offensive' that the Pope talked about a covenant between Christians and God coming as a result of a 'redemptive sacrifice of Jesus' which he considered 'in the post-Holocaust era ... an obscenity and an insult of the greatest proportions'.[4] This objection on the other hand was itself astounding to Christians because it touched on a basic tenet of Christianity. The Pope later clarified his earlier remarks by confirming that Israel was the people of God and a holy people. The short-lived row was dismissed by the Vatican as an example of over-sensitivity on the part of the Jews, since the Pontiff had not gone beyond the traditional Catholic interpretation of the Scriptures. The issue was, however, linked by the press with that of the convent, in which the Pope apparently did not want to intervene. It was considered by some Jews as evidence of the same negative attitude on the part of the Catholic Church.

Matters were not helped by the interviews given by Fr Dominik Wider and quoted by the *Guardian* on 17 August, who demanded that those people who sought the nuns' removal should build them a convent which, given Poland's desperate economic conditions, 'would require about eight years'.

Various Jewish delegations continued to visit Auschwitz and met with a hostile reaction from the local population. The *Jewish Chronicle* reported that a group of Knesset (Israeli Parliament) members were greeted by people shouting such things as 'Do we have the right to drive you out of Bethlehem because Jesus was born there? What right have you to tell us what to do here?'[5]

Sir Sigmund Sternberg, the Chairman of the International Council of Christians and Jews and a Papal Knight, sent a letter to Cardinal Macharski warning him that his decision indefinitely to postpone implementing the agreement would totally jeopardise all Christian-Jewish dialogue. Cardinal Macharski, replying on 22 August, stated 'The devastating effect produced by the substance and the form of the protest of some Jewish circles is so deep and so persistent in the social and religious awareness of the Poles, that it does not allow me to take a different opinion than that I expressed in my pronouncement.' Sir Sigmund replied immediately, pointing out that many Jewish organisations and individuals distanced themselves from Rabbi Weiss's actions.[6] Rabbi Marc Tannenbaum stated that he understood how the demonstrations 'touched off a furious reaction among Polish Catholics'.[7]

In a meeting with the Israeli Minister for Religious Affairs, Zevulun Hammer, Cardinal Macharski explained that he was not able to do anything while under pressure from Jewish organisations. The Poles could not understand why the nuns could not pray on the site and therefore 'a long educational process is required, as well as many talks with the Polish community, in an attempt to draw them closer to the Jewish people.' In an interview for *Polityka*, Hammer, whose parents were born in Poland, emphasised that he understood that good intentions lay behind the establishment of the convent and that he preferred negotiations to demonstrations. He considered the Holocaust to be an open wound and appealed for the silence of Auschwitz to be unbroken by prayer.[8] In another interview he stated that 'the living have no rights but only obligations towards those victims. We must find a way of understanding and compromise so that this tragedy does not become the seeds of conflict between our nations and religions'.[9]

In a meeting with Monsignor Lehmann, Chairman of the German Bishops' Conference in Warsaw, Bishop Muszyński, Chairman of the Polish Episcopate's Commission for Dialogue with Judaism, echoed Cardinal Macharski's sentiments by saying that given the historical role of the Catholic Church in Poland, it was 'practically impossible' to remove the cross standing in front of the convent.[10]

Cardinal Glemp's Homily Causes Outrage

The biggest controversy surrounded a homily delivered by the Primate of Poland, Cardinal Józef Glemp, at the Jasna Góra Monastery in Częstochowa on 26 August. A part of this homily (which was rumoured to have been drafted by Professor Maciej Giertych), was devoted to the dialogue with the Jews. After acknowledging the complexities of Polish-Jewish relations throughout the centuries, he raised the issue of the convent at Auschwitz.

> Life, however, does not favour neat classifications, and relations between people fall into categories other than just friend or foe. In our country, this is especially true of the Jewish nation, which was never just a neighbour, but a member of the household and which through its distinctness both enriched us and caused us difficulties ...

> Alongside the Jewish innkeeper who induced the peasant to drink, alongside the Jews who propagated communism, there were among the Israelites people who gave Poland their talent and their lives. We were not indifferent to each other. For this reason manifestations of anti-polonism and anti-semitism were possible. In order to understand the complexity and pervasiveness of Polish-Jewish problems let us ask ourselves: Has there been hostility towards Jews and have anti-Jewish disturbances occurred in Poland? They have. Have there been Jewish businessmen who disregarded and despised Poles? There have. Were there Jews during the occupation who collaborated and who did not live up to the heroic defenders of the ghetto? There were. Have there been periods of silence in Poland over the suffering of Jews and their victimization? There have. Have there been Poles who died saving Jewish lives? There have. The memory of the 50th anniversary of the Second World War puts us on the same side of the barricade, on the side of destruction and death. Jews, Gypsies, Poles – in the Nazi grand strategy these were peoples condemned to extermination – but according to different plans and on different scales. The Polish intelligentsia, for example, was the first to be destroyed. A common fate linked the persecuted. At the Polish military cemetery at Monte Cassino alongside the crosses marking Catholic graves are inscriptions with the star of David – all are Polish soldiers. Among the mass graves of murdered Polish officers at Katyn there are most certainly also

Jewish graves. The brotherhood of common martyrdom and common ashes is of profound significance. ...

Many Jews immersed themselves in Polish culture and in Christianity and the cross which stands above their graves did not deprive them of love of their nation.

Why, then, has the problem of Oświęcim and the Carmelite Convent arisen? Why has it suddenly erupted, 40 years after the crematorium fires have been extinguished? These questions trouble many of us when we speak about the peace which should wipe out the consequences of war. I would like to broach this subject in all humility and with the desire for unity. It has become so fraught with questions, dialogue is necessary. A dialogue to explain difficult matters systematically and not to present demands. We have our faults with regard to the Jews, but today one should like to say: my dear Jews, do not speak to us from the position of a nation raised above all others and do not present us with conditions that are impossible to fulfil.

The Carmelite sisters who live next to the camp in Auschwitz desired, and desire to be a sign of that human solidarity which embraces the living and the dead. Do you not see, esteemed Jew, that protesting against them disturbs the emotions of all Poles, and our hard-earned sovereignty? Your power lies in the mass media which is at your disposal throughout many countries. Do not let this power serve to disseminate anti-polonism. Recently, a squad of seven Jews from New York attacked the convent in Auschwitz. Admittedly the sisters were not killed nor was the convent destroyed because they were restrained – but do not designate them heroes. Let us maintain a civilized attitude. Let us identify certain simplified and muddled issues. Let us differentiate between Oświęcim-Auschwitz where mainly Poles and people of other nations perished, from Brzezinka-Birkenau a few kilometres apart where most of the victims were Jews. Let us differentiate next between the secular and the theological levels. Let the new doctrine on the presence or absence of God at the place of sacrifice be explained and clear to all those believing in God, and let it not become a political tool in people's hands, particularly of non-believers.

Let us who honour Mary of Nazareth and share many sacred places with you, Jews, begin the dialogue in sincerity and truth. Without anti-polonism there will be no anti-semitism here either. We wish for you that on the holy land of Palestine no one should stone you, that the sound of gunfire should cease, that no one should die from a bullet, and that peace-*shalom* will be with you.

The homily provoked an immediate and unprecedented response from the Polish press. The Solidarity daily *Gazeta Wyborcza* printed a tough response from its deputy editor the well-known Catholic intellectual, Krzysztof Śliwiński, on 28 August, which was the most critical public statement about a Primate ever to appear in a non-Communist, Catholic medium. Śliwiński talked about the feelings of regret and pain with which the Primate's homily had been greeted. He considered the timing to be most unfortunate and the words potentially offensive and truly injurious to the Jews. He considered that no one had the right to question the sincerity of the Jews who objected to the nuns' presence in Auschwitz or to consider their protests to be effects of political or journalistic manipulation exercised in bad faith. The same issue of *Gazeta Wyborcza* printed a message from the Pope on the occasion of the fiftieth anniversary of the outbreak of the Second World War in which he particularly singled out for condemnation 'the planned barbarity of which the victims were the Jewish people', stating that it would forever remain a sign of disgrace for mankind and appealed to everyone to renounce prejudice and combat all forms of racism. The appearance of both Śliwiński's condemnation of the Primate and the Pope's pro-Jewish appeal in the widely-read and respected national Solidarity daily was a clear sign of what the opposition thought about the issue. On 30 August Lech Wałęsa referred to the dispute as 'a shame and disgrace' and called for the creation of an international commission to resolve it peacefully. On the other hand, the Catholic nationalistic weekly *Ład* (10 September 1989) criticised Śliwiński's article for 'lecturing the Primate'. Its author, Andrzej Siemıanowski, suggested that even the removal of the nuns would not satisfy some Jews. He then accused those who broke into the convent of violence which 'injured the hearts of Polish people', because 'the attack on the convent at Auschwitz was more than an attack, it was also the profanation of a sacred place'.

The Primate's homily caused the Rabbi Pinhas Menahem Joskovicz, appointed Chief Rabbi of Poland in May 1989, to pull out in protest of the three-day prayer for peace in Auschwitz and Warsaw organised by the Polish church to commemorate the 50th anniversary of the outbreak of the Second World War. The Rabbi publicly requested that the Primate retract his homily from Częstochowa. Rabbi Joskovicz said 'I cannot believe Cardinal Glemp thought what he was reported to have said. He must have thought something else.'[11] The prayers at Auschwitz were also boycotted by other representatives of Polish Jewry and no major Jewish organisations attended. An Italian Bishop present, Pietro Rossano, Secretary of the Vatican division for non-Christian religions, repeated a statement made recently by the Pope that hostility towards Jews was unchristian. In a clear attempt to elicit a modification from Cardinal Glemp, he stated 'I am sure that this is in the heart and mind of the Primate of Poland, but I cannot correct him'.[12]

On 29 August, Cardinal Decourtray issued a statement in which he claimed that it was 'improbable that the meaning of Cardinal Glemp's statement was such as conveyed to the public. The Polish primate and bishops cannot be accused of anti-semitism which they condemn.' He then continued, with some uncertainty, by saying 'as far as I know, the Geneva agreement ... has not been annulled'.

Cardinal Glemp attempted to explain his position in an interview with the Rome daily *La Republica* in which he made additional statements which further complicated the issue and antagonized both international Jewish and Catholic opinion. Cardinal Glemp asserted that the nuns' praying near the wall of the concentration camp could not offend anybody and could not understand why devotion to 'a life of prayer near the place where Christians were martyred' could offend Jewish feelings. Besides, he considered moving the nuns by 500 yards to be irrational and an infringement of their property rights. 'Suppose I came to your house and said: you have to move this wardrobe. You rightly would respond – that's stupid, this is my property.' Furthermore, it would be a scandal to expel the nuns, he said, because they would have to live in tents.

When questioned about the Geneva agreement, the Primate stated that it had not been signed by competent people, and that Cardinal Macharski did not understand the situation of the people, and that the Cardinals of Paris, Lyon and Brussels also lacked understanding of the issue and were not competent to decide such an agreement, which could not be signed 'by any old cardinal'. The agreement had been signed hastily and the Primate demanded its renegotiation and demanded the participation of Poles in this process, since Cardinal Macharski alone represented only the Church of Cracow, and the problem itself concerned wider issues.[13]

Cardinals Castigate Glemp

This interview provoked a strong reaction, reported in Poland, from the three foreign cardinals concerned who issued a curt joint statement on 3 September.

> If the Jewish delegation at the meeting in Geneva, chaired by Theo Klein, the Chairman of the European Jewish Congress, is not competent, then who is competent?
> And if four cardinals, of whom one is the Archbishop of Cracow, are not adequately qualified to represent the Catholic side, then who is thus qualified?
> The camp in Auschwitz lies within the Cracow archdiocese. According to Church law, it is primarily the Archbishop who exercises full authority there. The cardinals who have joined him, belong to those nations of the West which were the main victims of Nazi barbarity.'

They restated that Cardinal Glemp could only be speaking for himself, especially since he had until then considered Cardinal Macharski to be the only person responsible in this matter. They ended by saying that the agreement must be fulfilled.

Cardinal John O'Connor, the Archbishop of New York, said at a news conference on 29 August that he was shocked by the remarks made by Cardinal Glemp and that he wished that the Polish Church hierarchy would implement the formal commitment of Geneva. Cardinal O'Connor felt that, as a result of Cardinal Glemp's distress at the New York Jewish community, the blame for the controversy was being transferred to the Jewish community.[14]

Speaking in the Netherlands, Cardinal Simonis of Utrecht, although agreeing in principle that the convent should be relocated, said that the delay was caused 'by very fanatical Jews. When one interferes with the Cross, one interferes with the Poles too.'[15]

Meanwhile, the Carmel in Auschwitz was joined by five more nuns. As the Mother Superior commented, 'The future is in the hands of God.'

Theo Klein regarded this to be 'an internal matter of the Catholic Church, even of the Polish Catholic Church ... I think that Cardinal Glemp's statements were not devoid of Polish domestic political considerations.'[16]

Glemp Accused of Anti-Semitism

Members of the American Jewish community came out with strong criticism of Cardinal Glemp. Rabbi Marvin Hier, Dean of the Wiesenthal Centre, called the Primate's remarks 'insulting and unworthy of a man of the cloth' and thought that he wanted to de-Judaize the Holocaust.[17] Michael Lerner, the editor of a liberal Jewish monthly *Tikkun*, appealed to President Bush and the American Congress to withhold American economic and political support for Poland and other East European countries until they dealt effectively with anti-semitism.[18] Other Jews also appealed to the US government to stop economic aid and to Jews not to travel to Poland. Glen Richter, one of the seven American Jews who climbed over the convent fence, insisted that their action was 'peaceful in intent'. In Belgium Jewish[19] organizations expressed 'dismay and indignation' about the homily. The Simon Wiesenthal Centre in Los Angeles stated that the Polish government had the ultimate authority over Auschwitz and that it must force the Church to change its stance.[20] The World Jewish Congress appealed to the new Solidarity-led government to disassociate themselves from the Cardinal's remarks. There was some speculation that the new Prime Minister, Tadeusz Mazowiecki, as a devout Catholic himself, would not do anything against the Primate. This kind of insinuation misjudged the complexity of religious life in Poland and revealed ignorance of Mazowiecki's character. Theo Klein, who led the Jewish Delegation in Geneva, considered Cardinal Glemp's pronouncement to be similar to those made by churchmen in the Middle Ages. He compared the Primate's reference to Jewish control of the media with similar statements made earlier by the Nazis.[21]

Lord Jakobovits, the Chief Rabbi of Britain, found Cardinal Glemp's statement incredible and 'grossly offensive ... Speaking, as he does, from the slaughterhouse of 3 million Polish Jews and 3 million other Jews herded to Poland for liquidation from all over Europe, the Cardinal could have been expected to show some special sensitivity to Jewish anguish and thus to contribute to better brotherly relations in the future.'

The Director of the Council of Christians and Jews, Canon Jim Richardson, considered the Primate's remarks about the Jews threatening the lives of the nuns to be 'a reintroduction of the blood libel'.[23]

Wishing to find a solution, the Prime Minister of Italy, Giulio

Andreotti, in an interview published on 28 August in the weekly *L'Espresso* expressed the opinion that the Jews were wrong to desire the expulsion of the nuns. But, he added, if 'a charitable gesture ought to be made towards Jewish sensibility, then it should be made'. He offered to place the convent by the Ardeatin Caves near Rome where in 1944 the Nazis shot 335 inhabitants of the city, including several dozen Jews. Objecting to this, Tulia Zevi said that the problem would not have existed had the commitments been honoured and that 'building a convent where martyrs of different faiths and convictions rest together evokes the missionary harshness of frontier Catholicism.'[24]

The Waldensian Church, the first proto-Protestants of the 12th century, regarded as heretical by Rome, was reported as totally supporting the Jews on the issue.

Cardinal Glemp's homily was widely quoted in the Western press which by and large described it as anti-semitic. *Le Monde* of 29 August asked a rhetorical question: 'Did not Cardinal Glemp miss a good opportunity to shut up?' The front page article contrasted Cardinal Glemp's pronouncements unfavourably with a statement by John Paul II issued on the occasion of the fiftieth anniversary of the outbreak of war. In his apostolic letter, the Pope stated firmly that 'enmity, or worse, hatred towards Judaism are in complete contradiction to the Christian vision of human dignity. I wish to strongly reaffirm this here.' He continued: 'The planned barbarity pursued relentlessly against the Jewish people, victims of the Final Solution, remains as a shame for humanity forever ... More than others, the Jews of Poland experienced this calvary. What was done to them in the camps of Auschwitz, Majdanek or Treblinka, surpasses in horror anything humanly conceivable.'

At the same time, Cardinal Glemp found some supporters outside Poland. Bernard Antony, a European Deputy for the French *Front National* of Le Pen declared that Cardinal Glemp's homily filled him with joy, and considered international reactions to it to be similar to those suffered by Le Pen in France (*Le Monde* 1 September). Andrew Brown writing in the *Independent* looked for a charitable explanation for the Primate's homily. He considered Cardinal Glemp 'despite appearances, a little ashamed of some earlier passages in Polish treatment of the Jews'. Moreover, he did not think his remarks could be 'properly described as anti-semitic. His denunciations, by turn hurt and hectoring, are of "anti-Polandism". And Jewish sentiment *is* largely hostile to Poland.'[25] Joanna Fraser, writing to the *Independent*

defended the Primate, although she considered him to be undiplomatic. Within Poland, the Polish Catholic Social Union issued a
declaration stating that it felt at one with Primate Glemp's homily
concerning, among other things, dialogue with the Jews. The organisation, formed in 1981, sat on the fence between supporting the
communist government and representing some nationalistic Catholics. It was supported by the Primate, but never had the support of
the Pope. Even when he was Archbishop of Cracow, he refused to
give audiences to the Catholic activists who later became prominent
members of this organisation.

The Press Discusses Polish-Jewish History

The interview was followed by a number of articles and letters appearing in a variety of papers. Antony Polonsky, a professor of
history at the London School of Economics, and President of the
Institute for Polish-Jewish Studies in Oxford, pointed out in a letter
to the *Jewish Chronicle* that the Jewish community should support
those moderate voices in Poland which were trying to resolve the
conflict peacefully. This could be done only 'by keeping cool heads
and refraining from ill-considered and counterproductive emotional
demonstrations, such as the shameful incursion of Rabbi Weiss and
his followers into the nunnery'. He stressed, nevertheless, that the
commitment made by the Church should be kept.[28]
Many letters dwell on Polish-Jewish history in general. Thus there
were numerous polemics about the extent of Polish anti-semitism
which Rabbi Sidney Brichto, Executive Vice-President of the Union
of Liberal and Progressive Synagogues, thought the country had
'borne for centuries'.[29] In reply, others pointed out that Poland was a
refuge for the Jews throughout the early modern period, and some
claimed that there was no anti-semitism in Poland at all. Many Jews
holding official positions, including Hayim Pinner, Secretary
General of the Board of Deputies of British Jews, singled Poland out
as a place where the Jews were not treated as equals and where they
suffered discrimination.
The debate even reached the *Evening Standard* in which Nigella
Lawson, while professing to understand the nuns' good intentions,
criticized the Church's war record towards the Jews and advised the
nuns to show more respect for Jewish sensibilities.[30] Responding to
the above, Father Cunningham considered their presence in

Auschwitz 'in an essentially Catholic country' to be 'reasonable and sensible'.[31]

Most of the Jewish responses and Polish reactions to them showed a rather poor and very selective knowledge of history. Both sides found it much easier to take a narrow nationalistic attitude.

Polish Catholics Attempt to Limit the Damage

On 6 September, the Episcopate's Commission for Dialogue with Judaism issued a statement defending the position of Cardinal Macharski by saying that in the process of implementing the agreement, difficulties, polemics, quarrels, and violent protests had begun to emerge which had become a serious threat to the very idea of the Centre. In these circumstances, the Cracow Metropolitan had felt obliged to issue [his] statement. Strangely enough, the Polish Commission for Dialogue with Judaism did not consider indefinite postponement of the relocation of the nuns to be contrary to the earlier position of the Episcopate on the issue! Bishop Muszyński still considered that there was 'an urgent need' to build the Centre for Information, Education, Meetings and Prayer as agreed in Geneva. His statement regretted that the 'idea of the Centre did not meet with due interest and understanding on the part of the Jewish side' and appealed for talks 'in the spirit of the Geneva meetings' which would make it possible to 'find realistic opportunities for constructing the Centre'.

The following day, the new Catholic Prime Minister of Poland, Tadeusz Mazowiecki, said in a letter addressed to Sir Sigmund Sternberg but made public, that the Poles 'remember the untold suffering of the Jewish people whose each and every member stands unequalled among all martyrized nations'. The *Jewish Chronicle* called these remarks 'unprecedented', but speculated that the pro-Jewish stance of Mazowiecki might be due to his having Jewish grandparents who converted to Catholicism.[32] There seems to be a view in some Jewish circles that any Pole sympathetic to the Jewish people must have some Jewish ancestor.

In reality, the pronouncements of Cardinal Glemp caused great unease among many prominent Catholic figures, who nevertheless found it difficult to attack the Primate directly in view of the respect attached to his official position. There was a widespread feeling that the hierarchy of the Polish Catholic Church was becoming isolated from Catholics in the rest of Europe.

Jews in Poland Criticize the Primate

On 9 September *Polityka* published an article by Konstanty Gebert, a well-known independent Jewish journalist, 'A Little Less at Home', in which he demanded that the nation openly disassociate itself from the views of the Primate. Gebert declared himself to be a Polish citizen, but of 'a Poland without religious and racist bigotry, a Poland of solidarity and Solidarity'. Even before the Primate's statement which he considered to be a summary of the 'subsoil on which Polish anti-semitism regenerates itself', there were signs of intolerance and division between 'us' and 'them', and inconsistent attitudes on the part of Church officials who, since the suspension of the implementation of the Geneva agreement by Cardinal Macharski, seemed to be showing signs of ill will. Gebert quoted Father Musial with praise. 'One should stress here that the Catholic side did not enter into dialogue with the Jews with the idea of a tender already in mind. It was a sincere dialogue, taken up in the spirit of love and respect for the partner.' This dialogue occured, according to Gebert, because the Church understood that, since Catholic prayer in the place of extermination offended the religious feelings of the victims' descendants, 'it could not be pleasing to our mutual God'. 'How come seven demonstrators managed to make the Church change its attitude?' he asked. Although Gebert did not support the actions of Rabbi Weiss, he considered them a response to provocation on the part of the Church which had been dragging its feet for two and a half years. Cardinal Macharski regarded the demonstration as a justification *ex post factum* for the inertia of the Church. It was difficult to see any good will in this. Gebert recognised that Cardinal Glemp's pronouncement was representative of the attitudes and feelings of many Poles who did not understand the essence of the Geneva agreement and were therefore ready to consider Jewish claims to be an illegal interference in Polish affairs. 'It is also true that Poland often has unfair accusations levelled at her from the Jewish side which makes it easier for the Poles to reject even those accusations which are in some measure justified.' He considered the knee-jerk reaction of some Poles in defence of the Primate to be inappropriate, because criticism of some pronouncements of a high member of the Church hierarchy was not necessarily synonymous with an attack on the Church. He ended by saying that he felt less at home in Poland and wondered how many people shared his feelings and how many were pleased by his 'homelessness'.

118

In over 20 letters which followed Gebert's article most Polish readers expressed their solidarity with and understanding of his position. One letter from an inhabitant of Oświęcim complained that the Church authorities had not informed the local Catholics about their negotiations and agreements, nor bothered to explain Jewish objections to praying on the site. The author did however, object to the behaviour of Rabbi Weiss – a sentiment shared by Gebert. Krzysztof Poklewski-Koziełł, imitating the Primate's legalistic approach to the problem, wrote a letter in which he stated that, as a lawyer, he considered it totally unacceptable unilaterally to break an agreement because of an 'escapade by a few American fanatics'. If Cardinal Macharski considered the relocation schedule to be unrealistic, why did he sign the agreement? Poklewski-Koziełł was much upset that an Archbishop could first not fulfil his promise and then break it. He criticised Cardinal Glemp for supporting Cardinal Macharski and for imputing attempted felony to Rabbi Weiss.

Two or three letters were openly anti-semitic, defending the Primate as 'a wise and balanced man' who had a right to act as he did, because 'this is our home, our land and our country'. Jews were accused of bringing communism to Poland together with the Red Army. One compared the treatment of Palestinians in Israel to that faced by the Poles from the hands of the Gestapo and NKVD. 'For the Poles,' said the author, 'Nazi Germany, and the Judeo-Communism of Moscow and her Polish collaborators are the same thing'.

On 10 September representatives of all Jewish communities in Europe affiliated with the European Jewish Congress, during their annual general meeting, voted a resolution deploring the failure to implement the Geneva agreement and stated that what was intended as an act of understanding and reconciliation had degenerated into a display of prejudice and intolerance. Dr Lionel Kopelowitz, the President of the EJC, said that Jewish suffering was being wilfully ignored.

Speaking in France, the French Prime Minister Michel Rocard blamed the former communist government of Poland for the problem, because for years it had attempted to include Auschwitz in the UNESCO World Heritage List and then, a few months after this classification was obtained, it had given part of the site to the Carmelites: 'It was a contradictory decision, a serious mistake.'

On 12 September 1947 leading intellectuals, including some Jews and well-known priests, signed an appeal which appeared in *Tygodnik Powszechny* (24 September 1989), in which they talked about 800 years of Polish-Jewish relations, acknowledging their darker chapters, but strongly supports the idea of ending the controversy by building the Centre outside the camp.

Cardinal Glemp Attempts to Clarify His Position

On the same day Cardinal Glemp, who had just been forced to cancel his trip to the United States because of the risk of Jewish demonstrations and opposition from many American Catholics, made a speech at the Catholic University of Lublin to the congress of Polish theologians, part of which was devoted to Polish-Jewish relations.[33] After discussing *Shoah* as a theological problem, he pointed out that it contained some ideological elements, and that 'ideology is always an instrument of various political games'. The issue of the Carmel which he considered to be 'inconspicuous' had caused much indignation. He claimed to respect the attitudes and feelings of the Jews but wanted them to understand the feelings of Polish Catholics too. He considered the conflict over the convent to be both legal and ethical. He responded to the accusations of broken promises or agreements by saying that:

> the document which resulted from the meetings at Geneva does not constitute an agreement. Obligations can only follow proper agreements in which those involved commit themselves to things possible. There can be no proper agreement if only one side ... is burdened by it. The obligations must be realizable. From the ethical standpoint, we do not retract that which really serves to solve the conflict, including the emotional one. However, this must be done in a dignified manner, in a manner which guarantees observance of the law and of correct conduct. The other ethical point concerns the expulsion of the Carmelite nuns – we cannot simply say: "we are moving you". The sisters have their rights after all, legally granted, hereto unquestioned. The Church cannot evict, taking upon itself the responsibility of violating the law and the human dignity of these women, who have a right to live in that place. Our stance is that of calm and honest appraisal of these difficult questions, and we do not pre-judge the outcome. But this cannot be done with shouting and noise and very harmful accusations. The truth is that here in Poland, despite this pressure, there is no anti-semitism. Truly there is not.

In an attempt to clarify some issues and to show that not all Polish Catholics shared the outlook of Cardinal Glemp, Professor Jacek Woźniakowski, whose mother sheltered Jews during the war, gave a long interview to *Le Monde* on Polish-Jewish relations.[39] He restated that Polish Catholics were surprised about the reaction to the establishment of the convent because no one had objected to two similar establishments: a parish church in Birkenau and a Salesian convent in the vicinity of Auschwitz – and pointed out that the latter, not being contemplative, might have been considered even more objectionable. Moreover, in 1978 a parish priest of Oświęcim notified the Social and Cultural Association of Jews in Poland that the inhabitants of the town wanted to pray for the martyred Jews near the camp. The place of prayer was already marked by a cross. The association thanked the priest without making any comment. He considered the main problem to be the differences in ways of honouring the dead between the Jewish and the Christian communities. The communion of saints essential for Catholics (although difficult to accept for many other Christians), may also incense the Jews. Woźniakowski pointed out that regardless of the respective number of Jewish and Polish victims of the camp, it was difficult for the families of the Polish victims to learn that they may not have the right to pray for them in the way that they wished. At the same time, he stressed that the Poles must fulfil their obligations from Geneva, regardless of their possible formal deficiencies. 'The first gesture of good will should be made by Polish Catholics to manifest their comprehension of the immeasurable horror of the *Shoah*.'

On 15 September the Secretariat of the Polish Primate announced that a satisfactory solution to the financial problem of building the Centre had been found during talks with Zygmunt Nissenbaum – Chairman of the Nissenbaum Foundation, and a Jewish philanthropist of Polish origin, but not considered to be a representative of the Jewish community.

Shamir Declares Poles Inborn Anti-Semites

In early September, Itshak Shamir, the Israeli Prime Minister, when asked about his comments on Polish anti-semitism, remarked that 'Poles imbibe anti-semitism with their mothers' milk. This is something with which their tradition, their mentality is deeply imbued.' He compared it to Polish loathing of Russia 'the two things are not connected, of course, but that, too, is something very deep, like their hatred of the Jewish people. Today though, there are elements in Poland which have been cleansed of anti-semitism.'

The remarks of the Israeli Prime Minister caused a furious row amongst Polish communities around the world. Faced with this criticism, Shamir refused to retract but Yosef Ahimeir, the head of his office, attempted to make a distinction implying that they referred only to the past and not to the present and future. Shamir apparently wanted to 'develop warm ties and full diplomatic contacts with the Polish people and government'. Despite the positive attitude towards Israel on the part of the new Solidarity-led government, these remarks slowed down the process of re-establishing diplomatic links by a few months.

On 15–17 September *Gazeta Wyborcza* responded to the remarks made by Shamir. *Gazeta's* editor, Adam Michnik, the much respected ex-opposition leader of Jewish origin, called Shamir's statement untruthful, provocative, offensive to the entire Polish nation, insulting to Polish democracy and a gift to anti-semites. Michnik then criticised the violation of the Geneva agreement, the assault on the convent by Rabbi Weiss, the homily of Cardinal Glemp, and the Primate's nationalistically oriented adviser, Professor Maciej Giertych. The article ended with an appeal to 'remember that no hatred – neither anti-semitic, nor anti-Polish – can be "imbibed with a mother's milk". Hatred is always a product of our own stupidity and immorality.'

The same issue of *Gazeta Wyborcza* carried an interview with Mordekhai Palzur, Head of the Israeli Interest Section in Poland, in which he tried to explain the remarks made by Itshak Shamir, greeted with indignation by most Poles. He explained that Shamir's father was believed to have been murdered by his Polish colleagues after he escaped from a transport on the way to a death camp. Palzur therefore distinguished between Shamir the politician who was much interested in normalising the relationship with Poland and keen to visit the country, and Shamir the person.

Polish Intellectuals Despair

Interviewed by the Polish Section of Radio Free Europe in Munich, Czesław Miłosz and Leszek Kołakowski, the prominent historian of philosophy, urged the nuns to move. Miłosz emphasized that in the name of good relations between faiths and for the good of the country, the nuns should show tact and move – a solution which would be greeted with great applause by Catholic public opinion in the United States. Kołakowski despaired that amongst both Jews and Poles there seemed to be a demand for a monopoly of martyrology. He considered 'reaffirming one's tribal exclusivity on the ashes of countless martyrs, victims of genocide' to be a lamentable state of affairs. Marek Edelman, the last surviving commander of the Warsaw Ghetto Uprising and a prominent figure in Solidarity, considered Cardinal Glemp's pronouncements to be very unwise and damaging for Poland. He admitted that the Jews may have historically rooted prejudices about the cross: 'If someone has prejudices, then he who is wiser should give way. In such a political situation Cardinal Glemp should be the wiser one.' In an interview Edelman gave to *La Republica* of 30 August 1989, he declared that the views of Cardinal Glemp were not representative of the views held by the Polish clergy in general, especially outside the hierarchy. He pointed out that there were many open-minded priests closely associated with Solidarity. He regretted that Cardinal Glemp had not shown the statesmanship required of a person in his political position, taking into account the role of the Church in Poland.

Polish Catholics Put Pressure on the Primate

On 17 September *Tygodnik Powszechny* published an interview with Cardinal Glemp conducted by Jacek Woźniakowski, an eminent intellectual and director of the Catholic publishing house *Znak*. The Primate suggested that the Geneva agreement should be renegotiated, but accepted Woźniakowski's interpretation that the new agreement would not be in any substantial way different from the old one:

> Renegotiation does not necessarily mean that the agreement already reached will be invalidated, only that it will be perfected. From this point of view, the Geneva negotiations had a number of faults, including the fact that both sides were unequal. As I understand it, the Jewish side was represented by a strong, cohesive national group, and the Catholic side – to use a sociological term – by an informal denominational group. This does not at all mean that I do not appreciate the enormous

amount of work done on these difficult issues by the three cardinals or the significance of the position they took.

Cardinal Glemp defended his previous position, taking his usual narrow legalistic stance, which, he claimed, had forced him to take a variety of opinions about the issue into account, and he complained that some of his phrases had been misinterpreted by the press. Woźniakowski, quoting the rights and duties of lay Catholics to participate in the decision-making process of the Church, put considerable pressure on the Primate by insisting on the speedy implementation of the Geneva agreement and the immediate beginning of work on the new Centre. He emphasised that moving the nuns by a few hundred yards was no tragedy and that 'God would hear their prayers just as well from their new location'. Woźniakowski was primarily concerned about the grave damage Poland's image was suffering in the eyes of the world. Cardinal Glemp concluded the interview by questioning how the uniqueness of the *Shoah* could be reconciled with 'the ordinary existence of Israel within the human family? I have the impression that Israel is still anxiously searching for this ordinary place' and he hoped that 'this exceptional nation would completely find its place in the family of all the peoples'. As *Gazeta Wyborcza* commented, the Primate had, in fact, accepted the relocation of the convent.

Cardinal Glemp is noted for his unfortunate choice of phrase. To refer to a group of four important cardinals as an 'informal denominational group' suggests some pique that he was not personally involved in the original negotiations. His opinion that Israel has not yet found its place in the family of the nations is at best puzzling and at worst patronizing.

Auberon Waugh, commenting on the Cardinal's predeliction for infelicitous turns of phrase, expressed his fears for Poland: 'Glemp's position as Primate is a crucial one ... and everything depends on a man who appears to have the political wisdom and tact of the proverbial bull in a china shop.'[35]

Some correspondents insisted that aid to the new Polish government should be linked to the successful conclusion of the rift over the convent because 'if Poland is allowed to repudiate its Auschwitz agreement it might believe it can do so with financial agreements.'[36] This statement, although mistaken, since the Solidarity led government had nothing to do with the Geneva agreements and the subsequent problems surrounding them, showed the impact of the Polish

Episcopate's vacillation on the general perception of Poland abroad. As Professor Piotr Słonimski, President of the Franco-Polish Solidarity Society and a relative of the famous Polish *Haskalah* (Jewish Enlightenment) figure Chaim Zelig Słonimski, remarked during his visit to Poland in the autumn of 1989:

> It is shocking that the head of the Church in Poland should express himself like an anti-semite. Cardinal Glemp's pronouncements on the affair of the Carmelites has cost Poland a billion dollars.
>
> The West has no time to analyse why Primate Glemp introduced the subject, whether it was a reckoning with 'Solidarity' and so on. It simply responds thus: the Poles have defeated communism, they have freedom, and anti-semitism appears. This could cool enthusiasm, just as 1968 completely compromised a 'good' communist – Gomułka.[37]

Confusion reigned amongst Jewish organisations about the appropriate response to the controversy. Theo Klein was reported as saying 'We have asked Jewish organisations to stop every kind of dialogue. The situation in Jewish communities and among Catholic people is such that we don't want to have dialogue now.'[38] This was immediately denied by Dr Riegner, co-chairman of the World Jewish Congress governing board. The officers of the Council of Christians and Jews postponed their visit to Italy which was to have included an audience with the Pope. However, the organisation's chairman, Sir Sigmund Sternberg, a firm believer in dialogue, refused to cancel his own meeting with the Pontiff.

CHAPTER 9

Resolution

The Decisive Intervention of the Vatican

On 19 September the Holy See issued a statement signed by Cardinal Willebrands, announcing the removal of the Convent in a way which could be understood only by people well-versed in the language of official Vatican pronouncements. In fact, the Jewish community did not at first grasp the significance of the Vatican's intervention. Willebrands's statement welcomed the communique of the Polish Episcopate of 6 September, mentioned above, and continued:

> The plan to establish a Centre of Information, Education, Meetings, and Prayer, which was anticipated by the Geneva Declaration of February 1987 is received with great pleasure. The Holy See is convinced that this Centre will contribute in a significant way to the development of good relations between Christians and Jews. Indeed, the Holy Father, in his address to the Jewish community in Vienna on 24 June 1988, expressed the hope that 'this Centre will bear rich fruit and will serve as a model for other countries'.
>
> The prayer and consecrated lives of the Carmelite sisters whose convent will, in a sense, be the heart of this Centre, will decidedly contribute to its success.
>
> The Holy See is prepared to contribute financially to support the completion of such an important, but costly project.

At that time Cardinal Glemp was paying a visit to Britain. In Bristol, which he visited in order to consecrate a Polish church, he stated that negotiations were under way to find the financial resources needed to pay for the construction of the new centre. Blaming the delay on various administrative and economic factors, he stated that the removal by force from Auschwitz of the nuns who had settled there legally was not acceptable. He described at length the history of the controversy and gave a somewhat insensitive critique of what he referred to as '*Shoah* theology'. He considered the problem of the Carmelites to have arisen because of the Jewish understanding of the Holocaust 'for Jews who believe, the theory of *Shoah* implies that God left them, deserted them, in this place of suffering.' He still maintained that although he supported the idea of the new ecumenical centre and that the nuns might eventually move, he would also accept their refusal to do so. He referred to the Geneva Agreement as 'wishful thinking'.[1]

Cardinal Willebrands's subtly-worded communique was as understandable to him as to any other Catholic. Upon hearing the news about the Vatican's communique, Glemp said 'That would provide a forceful solution to the problem'. Despite the obscure language of this pronouncement which spoke only about the pleasure with which the Vatican accepted the project to build the Centre and its willingness to contribute to it financially, Catholics realised that the Pope supported the removal of the convent. It was clear that the Pope had decided to impose his will on the Polish Episcopate. The manner in which this was done was highly unusual, as as it not normal for the Vatican publicly to overrule such a high dignitary of the Church, especially since the matter was not really within its jurisdiction.

The following day, 20 September, Cardinal Glemp retreated with dignity at a meeting at the Polish Embassy in London, attended by the Primate, his personal secretary and the Polish Ambassador on one side, and Sir Sigmund Sternberg the Chairman of the Council for Christians and Jews, Antony Polonsky, Edward Roche and Rabbi Tony Bayfield on the other. The leaders of the main Jewish organisations in Britain including the Board of Deputies of British Jews and the Chief Rabbi Jakobowits had refused to meet Cardinal Glemp because of the homily which had been delivered in August. Thus, although an agreement resulted from this meeting with prominent Jewish individuals, they were not in fact officially representing their community. This made it easier for the Cardinal to retract, since neither he nor the Jewish participants had played any role in the formulation of the original declaration in Geneva. Over dinner, Cardinal Glemp drafted a letter addressed to Sir Sigmund in which he stated that it was his 'intention that the Geneva Declaration of 1987 should be implemented'. He declared that he would like to 'work on a friendly dialogue between Christians and Jews'. In an attempt to justify his previous stance, he declared that until Sir Sigmund sent his messages to Poland 'I was unaware of the moderating voices, therefore I was glad that some of the shrill voices do not reflect the feelings of world Jewry and aggression is not part of Jewish philosophy. There has been a great deal of ill feeling and misunderstanding which we would like to clear up. We are a people of our word and we understand that the implementation of the Declaration can only take place in a tranquil atmosphere. It is essential not only to move the Convent outside the perimeter of the site, but also to set up the new cultural centre. This will help us to continue the dialogue which is so dear to us.' The then Polish Ambassador, Zbigniew Gertych, was instrumental in persuading the Primate of the desirability of signing the agreement. Harassed by the politically liberal Polish Catholics, overruled by the Vatican, faced with the strong disapproval of the Western Catholic hierarchy, virtually dis-invited by the American Episcopate from his planned grand tour of the States, Cardinal Glemp had no option but to bow down gracefully.

Commenting upon his decision, Cardinal Glemp admitted that the Church had made some mistakes. 'We actually were not aware that there would be such deep feelings on the part of Jews towards this place.' He said that the Church 'would have to explain in every Catholic parish the Jewish view that the only fitting memorial at a site where so many Jews were gassed and burnt is emptiness and silence.' He stated that he had changed his mind about the Geneva agreement during his visit to Britain and said that 'the Jews in London were very polite and nice and we reached some understanding'. This was in contrast to the 'unpleasant behaviour of some American Jews'.[2]

Relieved Response of the International Press

Cardinal Glemp's letter was immediately made public and resulted in a plethora of positive editorials in English, American, and other newspapers. The *Times* published an editorial written by Clifford Longley in which he stated that Cardinal Glemp 'unexpectedly accepted an olive branch offered to him at the last minute by a group of British Jewish leaders, and responded generously'. He considered that this breakthrough was possible because of the 'reserves of good will that still survive between Jews and Christians'. Praising the Polish Primate for understanding that 'the victims, of whatever faith, deserved better than that, from both sides', the *Times* said that 'it is a tribute to Cardinal Glemp's magnanimity that he has grasped this, and altered his position so speedily'.[3]

The *New York Times* published an editorial entitled 'Balm from the Vatican' which praised the Pope for intervening in the affair and inspiring his countrymen to take 'a more universal vision'. Acknowledging the role that the Polish Catholic Church played in the fight 'for freedom from foreign sponsored Communist dictatorship' the *New York Times* pointed out that in the fight to preserve national existence and identity, the Polish Church has sometimes behaved in an insular and parochial manner. It noted that there were those Poles such as Tadeusz Mazowiecki and John Paul II who share a broader vision. The editorial noted with approval that the Vatican's declaration was carefully worded and presented outwardly as a recommendation rather than an order, thus respecting 'the dignity of Poland's Catholic hierarchy'.[4]

The *Washington Post* in its editorial stated that 'the Vatican has lent its very considerable weight to a decent and enlightened agreement'. It considered the proposed solution to the problem to be a 'wiser and better response'.[5] Cardinal Glemp accepted this decision the next day and stated that it was his intention that the Geneva declaration should be implemented.

The Chief Rabbi of Britain, Lord Jakobovits, who did not wish to see the Cardinal during his visit to Britain, sent him a letter in which he praised his 'substantial contribution to the reestablishment of Catholic-Jewish harmony'.

The news was reported in many Polish papers. *Gazeta Wyborcza* of 22–24 September published a long article by Krzysztof Śliwiński, the title of which ('Rome has spoken, the matter is resolved') showed a great degree of satisfaction that the Vatican decided to intervene openly in the matter. Śliwiński pointed out that the construction of the Centre was only a matter of time, since for all Catholics the Pope's decision was final. The resolution of the conflict was to benefit everyone. *Gazeta* received over 300 letters expressing opinions about the controversy, over 100 of which disagreed with the liberal stance taken by the paper. Among these about 30 letters were openly anti-semitic.

Another Solidarity paper, *Tygodnik Solidarność* published two articles on 29 September. In 'The Carmelite Convent – Without Emotion', Fr Waldemar Chrostowski, stated that it was evident that Poles and Jews did not successfully deal with their common past and that mutual prejudices and aversions resurface very easily.

'There is no way to avoid the view that the postwar period – despite unquestionable changes brought about by Vatican II and the consolidation of the Jews in their own state – was not taken advantage of for a successful transformation in the thinking of members of both communities.'

On 21 September, Monsignor Muszyński wrote in a letter to Cardinal Willebrands that the Commission for Dialogue with Judaism had accepted his communique 'with deep gratitude and relief'. Referring to the problems with Catholic public opinion in Poland, Bishop Muszyński hoped that:

> the devotion and love felt for the Holy Father, the great authority of Cardinal J. Willebrands, and the *gravitas* of the Apostolic Capital's Commission for Religious Relations with Judaism, will mean that the communique will be accepted with great appreciation by a wide public in Poland, especially by Catholics.

A day later Cardinal Macharski issued a statement in which he also welcomed the communique, claiming that it confirmed his stand of 8 August 'that through dialogue it will be possible to find a solution preserving mutual respect and tolerance of one's own religious and national convictions.' Considering that Cardinal Macharski's position on 8 August was that the building of the Centre should be indefinitely postponed, it is difficult to see how the Vatican's decision could be interpreted as supportive.

Tygodnik Powszechny published on 1 October 1989 the text of Cardinal Willebrands's communique and a statement by Cardinal Macharski welcoming it and stating that the statement by the Holy See 'confirms the stand that I adopted on 8 August that through dialogue it will be possible to find a solution preserving mutual respect and tolerance of one's own religious and national convictions'. The same issue of *Tygodnik Powszechny* published an article by Father Adam Boniecki the editor of the Polish version of *L'Osservatore Romano* in which he reminded the readers that the key document of relevance to the controversy remained the Geneva Declaration. He also stated that the Pope made clear his commitment to the construction of a new Centre on 24 June 1988. At the height of the controversy the Pope had sent a message concerning Jewish suffering during the war. Thus the announcement that the Vatican was ready to sponsor the construction of the Centre was just a reassertion of its earlier position. The following week *Tygodnik Powszechny* published an article by Józef Tischner, Professor of Philosophy at the Pontifical Academy of Theology in Cracow and a friend of the Pope, examining the theological differences between Judaism and Christianity and the symbolism of the cross for both communities. Concentrating on the religious aspects of the controversy surrounding the convent, he sought to show that there were fundamental historical and religious differences which could not easily be resolved, despite the solution of the immediate conflict, but which required understanding and mutual respect.

Aftermaths of the Conflict

Kultura also contained a strong attack on the Primate by Krzysztof Wolicki who speculated about his political ambitions and suggested that Cardinal Glemp wanted to control developments in Poland by creating a mass Catholic political party with strong nationalistic undertones (the Primate wrote the Preface to the brochure by Roman Dmowski and is considered to share the latter's attitudes).[6] *Kultura* has been consistently critical of the attitudes and pronouncements of the Primate.

The articles about the convent continued even after the issue had been resolved. *Polityka* (30 September 1989) published an appeal by Stanisław Kania, chief specialist of the Central Committee for the Investigation of Nazi Crimes in Poland, in which he tried to explain the reasons for the emotional attitude of Jews towards the issue. He stated that, as the main victims of Auschwitz, the Jews had a special right to the camp and that this right had been consistently ignored by the Polish authorities, particularly between 1968 and 1978. The author demanded that the Polish population showed more respect for Jewish feelings and maintained silence at the place of the extermination of Jews.

On 5 October, in the aftermath of the resolution of the conflict, the Israel Diaspora Trust in London hosted a Catholic-Jewish meeting devoted to the controversy. It was chaired by Sir Sigmund Sternberg. Cardinal König, former Archbishop of Vienna, was one of the many notable figures attending, as was Lord Jakobovits the Chief Rabbi, Lord Weidenfeld and others. Lord Weidenfeld, introducing the debate, pointed out that the main lesson of the controversy was that both the Jewish and Catholic communities were pluralistic and thus there was no uniform line taken by either side.

Father McTurnan discussed the reactions of both Jews and Catholics which he judged unworthy and 'scandalous to unbelievers'. This view was shared by John Najmann who found it ironic that a Nazi death camp should have become 'the source of conflict between two victim nations, the Jews and the Poles'. Sidney Brichto commented that 'while the recognition of Catholic pluralism required Jews not to become euphoric over every utterance of good will, or to despair over every negative statement emanating from the Church, and vice versa, it was also necessary to appreciate that pluralism permitted extremes in both communities. It would be best for each community to deal with their own extremes, so that when Catholics or Jews were offended, they should not express their 'outrage' publicly, but should seek explanations, or the promise of moderate action from their associates in the other religious community.'

Rabbi Hugo Gryn, Senior Rabbi of the West London Synagogue, and others pointed out that the whole dispute was due to the mis-reading of symbols and that it was important to learn each other's symbols and the importance attached to them by both communities.

Insensitivity and lack of diplomacy on the part of the Jews was criticized by Sir Sigmund Sternberg who recalled Jewish demands that the cross at Auschwitz 'must go first' and their repeated demands 'when will the nuns go?' He was appalled by the attitude of some Italian Jews who had insisted that the Pope remove his cross before visiting the synagogue in Rome because it was a symbol of Jewish suffering. Rabbi Gryn's response to this was 'It would be like asking a Jew to uncircumcise himself before entering a church.'

Those who had attended the international conference 'Jews and Christians in a Pluralistic World' in November 1988 which attracted 62 participants from 14 different countries, were much impressed by the quality of the interfaith dialogue which took place and thought that the way forward lay in communicating the understanding which was achieved to the rank and file in both communities. This became more urgent as the dispute over the Carmel brought casualties. On 3 October 1989, Dr Joseph Wybran, Chairman of the Coordination Committee for Jewish Organisations in Belgium, involved in mediating in the dispute over the convent, was shot dead in an attack which was regarded by many as anti-semitic.

In Israel, as Reuter reported on 27 September 1989, 'an ancient Carmelite monastery was damaged in apparent protest over the Carmelite convent in Auschwitz.'

Tygodnik Powszechny of 12 November 1989 published a translation of an article about Jews and Christians in Auschwitz by Cardinal Willebrands which had appeared on 30 September in *L'Osservatore Romano*. In it the Cardinal tried to restate the position of the Vatican. He appealed for dialogue with the Jews, and attempted to quell Jewish fears and suspicions about the attitude of the Church.

However, the convent controversy refused to die out. In some Polish-American emigre papers an interview appeared with the Mother Superior of the Carmelite Convent, Sr Teresa. A retired US Air Force Colonel of Polish origin, Frances Winiarz, who visited Poland, met Sr Teresa, and reported her views on the controversy. She apparently claimed that neither Cardinal Macharski nor Cardinal Glemp had consulted the Sisters before the meeting in Geneva. She could not understand why the Jews objected to the convent since the nuns also offered prayers for those victims of Auschwitz who were Jewish. She regretted the fact that the Jews were creating such a problem for Poland at a time when the country was trying to become democratic again. She resented accusations of Polish anti-semitism and said 'Israel receives three billion dollars from the United States only because it is building a democratic country; however the daily press reports in detail how they are mistreating the Arabs. Greater anti-semites are hard to find.' She then reportedly described the post-war communist regime in Poland as being totally dominated by the Jews who had devastated the country, closed the churches, and attempted to introduce atheism into Poland. She ended up saying that the nuns were not going to move 'a single inch'.

Responding in the *Jewish Week*, Professor Alan Dershowitz rejected the prayers of the Carmelites as coming from 'an unreconstructed anti-semite'. He considered that Sr Teresa's remarks betrayed the hallmarks of traditional anti-semitism and suggested that Sr Teresa should 'pray for her own bigoted soul. God knows she needs it'. He noted that Sr Teresa's views were unfortunately not unusual among some Polish clergymen and that open-minded churchmen such as Cardinal Macharski and his predecessor Cardinal Wojtyła, the present Pope, had been 'sabotaged at every turn by some local Polish clerics who insist on repeating the old anti-semitic *canards*.'[8] The interview has become known in Poland although doubts have been expressed that the words attributed to Sr Teresa were accurately reported, especially in view of her war-time actions on behalf of the Jews.

In late November, Sir Sigmund Sternberg and Professor Antony

Polonsky went to Poland where they spoke at length to many people involved in the controversy. Cardinal Glemp assured them that the Church had acquired land for the new Centre and that plans had already been prepared by the architects. He emphasised, however, that the construction of the Centre was the responsibility of Cardinal Macharski as Archbishop of Cracow, and of Bishop Muszyński, the head of the Polish Episcopate's Commission for Relations with Judaism. Monsignor Muszynski informed them that the Chairman of the Catholic Intelligentsia Club in the town of Oświęcim actively supported the building programme, which had helped to calm the local population. On the stipulation of Prime Minister Mazowiecki, a committee to deal with all issues related to the Auschwitz-Birkenau complex had been formed. It was headed by Stefan Wilkanowicz and operated under the auspices of the Ministry of Culture. The main function of the committee was to rethink the role of the camp and to reorganise the Auschwitz Museum which has remained unchanged since Stalinist days. Sir Sigmund and Polonsky met a number of Polish Jews, many of whom were members of the newly-established Polish-Israeli Friendship Society. According to them, all the Jews were confident that the Geneva agreement would soon be implemented.

> They all stressed that irresponsible actions or statements by Jews abroad, with little knowledge of Polish conditions, enormously complicated their situation. The damage done by actions such as Rabbi Weiss's deplorable incursion into the Carmelite monastery was incalculable. According to Monika Krajewska [author of *Czas Kamieni* – an album documenting Jewish cemeteries in Poland], 'in one blow, an American publicity seeker and adventurist undid 10 years work in creating a better understanding between Poles and Jews'. Rumours that Rabbi Weiss might take Cardinal Glemp to court for slander were greeted with horror and alarm. Time and time again, Jewish leaders appealed to us to use our influence to persuade Western Jews to refrain from ill-judged and provocative statements or actions.[9]

Following this sentiment, Sir Sigmund Sternberg expressed his dismay about the action of an Israeli-based group – 'For My Brothers Keep Not Silence' – which announced a campaign to collect signatures and present them to the Pope and the Polish government, protesting at Polish and Roman Catholic attitudes towards the convent in Auschwitz. A full-page petition in the *Jerusalem Post* signed by Israel's two Chief Rabbis, leading mayors, and others protested against 'foot-dragging and failure to honour promises' to remove the convent. As Sir Sigmund pointed out, this action, taken after Cardinal Glemp had his change of heart, and at a time when the construction of the Centre was just about to begin, could only harm Israeli interests.

In December 1989, the press reported that Rabbi Weiss intended to sue Cardinal Glemp for slander. The Jewish response to the news was decidedly mixed.

In general, the controversy about the conflict was widely reported in most Polish papers. The Party papers were usually reluctant to take a clear stance, claiming that the issue should be resolved between the Church and the Jewish organisations, but they clearly relished the problems experienced by the Church. *Polityka* took a typically liberal line toward the controversy, while the hard line Party papers tried to form a Communist-nationalist alliance and criticised both the Jews and the Liberal Catholics. The Solidarity Press was critical and sometimes very outspoken against the Primate. The Catholic Press was divided between those papers which supported Cardinal Glemp and those (usually much more influential, like *Tygodnik Powszechny*) which attempted to explain the issue and strongly supported the implementation of the Geneva Declaration. Most Catholic groups and organisations took a liberal line and were considerably dissatisfied with the behaviour of Cardinals Macharski and Glemp. Many people realised that the conflict was damaging the image of Poland abroad at a time when it was necessary to gain international support. At the same time it would be wrong to assume that this concern with potential financial aid to Poland was the main or even the major reason for the criticism of the Primate, or even of Cardinal Macharski, expressed by the liberal intelligentsia, and the Solidarity circles. These groups appeared to be deeply embarrassed by the xenophobic, nationalistic nature of the Primate's pronouncements, and by the position taken by Cardinal Macharski, which was considered by many to be irrational and counter-productive.

The controversy revealed that the general public in Poland had little understanding of Jewish attitudes and objections. The newly emerged pluralistic community in Poland was able for the first time to express a variety of views openly. As a result they ranged from openly anti-semitic to strongly philo-semitic. The debate was largely influenced by the personality of the Primate who seems to have resented the fact that he was not a party to the original agreement reached in Geneva. One of the most unusual aspects of the debate was an open challenge to Cardinal Macharski's authority from the Primate, and the direct intervention of the Vatican which forced the Primate's hand. Never before had such internal disagreements been aired so publicly in the Polish media. The amount of public attention which the debate attracted was remarkable considering that the months between June and October 1989 constituted one of the most politically charged and euphoric periods in recent Polish history. The controversy took place simultaneously with the first semi-free elections since 1945, the negotiations leading to the formation of a new non-Communist coalition and the election of the first non-Communist Prime Minister in Eastern Europe since 1948. The amount of space devoted to the convent in the media and the involvement of leading figures in the attempts to mediate between the Jewish and Polish communities was a sign that the issue was regarded as central to Polish society at that time.

CHAPTER 10

Analysis

The Roots of the Controversy

The controversy surrounding the Carmelite Convent in Auschwitz
was provoked by a variety of factors which can be broken down into
the historical, legal, theological, political and personal.

The historical background to Polish-Jewish and Catholic-Jewish
relations in general has already been mentioned, as has the history of
Auschwitz-Birkenau camp. The importance which both Polish and
Jewish communities attach to the history of the Second World War,
the Holocaust, and Auschwitz has been discussed at length
elsewhere. It is enough to say that a struggle between two contradictory and powerful symbols lay at the core of the conflict. Their
significance related primarily to the issue of Polish and Jewish collective memory and the problem of national identity connected with it.
Since the war, Auschwitz has played a central role in the formation
of Jewish identity and an only slightly lesser role in the formation of
the Polish equivalent. The clash over the Carmel was so violent and
persistent because both communities felt that their past and future
identity was being directly threatened. Thus the issue was not about
the presence of a few nuns praying in an old dilapidated building. It
was about the Jews and the Poles being able to preserve two separate,
conflicting, and essential views of history grounded in the same
place. This not quite common past was of fundamental importance,
especially for the Jews who, as we have seen, divide their history into
'before' and 'after Auschwitz'.

Legal Problems

From a legal point of view, the problems involved Polish, international, and Church law. In July 1947 the government of the Polish
People's Republic declared the complex of Auschwitz-Birkenau
concentration and extermination camp to be a monument to the

137

martyrdom of the Polish nation and others, and established a museum there. From that moment the site became legally protected as an historic site. At least one Jewish commentator thought that the establishment of the convent in a building which, although outside the perimeter of the camp and used as a storage building, was nevertheless part of the museum complex, violated the legal status of the place because 'the decree of the Polish government speaks only of the *conservation* of the site, not of changing its character by its use as a place of worship by one particular faith'.

The second legal problem related to international law. The legal status of the camp after the site had been accepted in 1979 on a list of protected places by the World Heritage List of UNESCO was unclear. The Convention for the Protection of the World Cultural and National Heritage ratified by Poland in 1976 specified that:

> Each State Party to this Convention recognises that the duty of ensuring the identification, protection, conservation, presentation and transmission to future generations of the cultural and natural heritage referred to in Articles 1 and 2 and situated on its territory, belongs primarily to that State ... (Art. 4)[1]

Many people considered that the leasing of the old theatre building, which had been included in the plan attached to the formal application to UNESCO, to the nuns by the State violated this article. For them the establishment of a convent was not compatible with either protection or conservation. They argued that the building should be kept in its original state. This argument was weakened by the lack of interest in the building shown by the Jewish community before it became a convent. Was it because the Jews considered that the agricultural cooperatives preserved the 'original state' of the building by using it for storing goods just as the Nazis had done during the war? This is hardly believable. After all, Jewish objections were partially based on the fact that cans of Cyklon-B had been stored there. Nevertheless, the first Jewish objections to the convent came as early as December 1984. Professor Olgierd Czerner, Chairman of the National Committee of ICOMOS (International Council for the Protection of Historic Buildings and Places), was asked to investigate the accusation that the Polish government had ignored UNESCO regulations by allowing the convent to be established. According to one report, Professor Czerner had informed the government that the plans submitted to UNESCO included the building where the convent was located. The authorities apparently replied that they were not going to get involved in matters between the Church and the Jews.[2]

Rabbi Abraham Weiss pushed this point further by claiming that his intrusion into the convent could not be regarded as trespass because once the site had been included in the World Heritage List ·it ceased to be private property and became the property of all mankind. It is doubtful if this point of view would have been upheld by international law since even the UNESCO convention spoke about the state's sovereignty over the sites for which it had responsibility. A more moderate interpretation of this claim was given by B'nai B'rith which argued that the inclusion of the old theatre where the convent was located on the UNESCO list allowed for a degree of foreign control over it.

A similar legal issue was raised by the Belgian delegation which visited Poland in 1986 and claimed that everything related to Auschwitz-Birkenau had an international dimension. This view was rejected by the Polish government which stated that it had sovereignty over the territory and therefore total authority to take decisions without consulting any foreign body.

The further legal questions concerned the competence issue mentioned by Cardinal Glemp. Who, according to Church law, was competent to make decisions concerning the relocation of the nuns? Cardinals Decourtray, Danneels, and Lustiger stated in their angry response to Cardinal Glemp's challenge that they were competent to represent the Catholic side and that according to Church law the Archbishop of the diocese involved had primary and full authority over all matters related to it. Generally speaking, they were of course correct. In the case of the convent in Auschwitz, the matter was more complicated. First, the nuns belonged to a religious order which has its own authorities and chain of command. As such, they were subject to the orders of the Provincial of the Discalced Carmelites in Poland and to the Superior-General of the Order in Rome. In some cases, the ultimate arbiter is not the General of the Order, but the Congregation for Religious Orders and Secular Institutions. In the case of Poland, the situation is further complicated by the fact that the previous Primate, the late Stefan Cardinal Wyszyński, was granted personal authority over some religious orders by the Vatican. This was a highly unusual arrangement which lapsed with the Cardinal's death. However, Cardinal Glemp seems to have assumed that he still had this authority because apparently he was not informed otherwise. Thus when he challenged the competence of Cardinal Macharski he may have considered this to be legitimate. It is not clear who should negotiate on behalf of the Polish Roman Catholic Church over an issue which may be considered to be of national importance. If one assumes that the convent was not just a local problem in one of the dioceses, it appears that Cardinal Macharski would need the approval of the Polish Episcopate and its Chairman, the Primate. Ultimately, it may be that neither Cardinal Macharski nor Cardinal Glemp had full authority over the nuns. This rested with the Father-General of the Carmelites, Monsignor Philippe Sainz de Baranda. Father Dominik Wider, the Provincial of the Polish Carmelites, may have been right when he said in June 1989 that the convent would be moved only on Vatican orders. On the other hand, the Superior General had already made his feelings about the issue absolutely clear in January of that year. In a letter to Cardinal Decourtray of 19 January 1989 he said:

> Since the Geneva agreement of 23 February 1987 has been signed by a Catholic delegation in the name of the Church, the implementation of all its points is beyond discussion and as a consequence the Discalced Carmelites of Auschwitz were obliged to agree to the relocation foreseen in the agreement. I immediately informed the General Council of this at the session held on 19 January 1989 and the Superior of the Carmelite province in Poland. The Superior of the Polish province although personally unfavourably inclined to the relocation of the sisters, accepted my opinion and will loyally, after which he informed both Cardinal Macharski and the Discalced Carmelites of it, which they accepted with great love of the Church and the Pope ...'[3]

As the first sentence of the General's statement indicates, he knew that Cardinal Macharski had exceeded his competence by agreeing to the removal of the convent, which ultimately lay outside his jurisdiction. However, despite the fact that his personal authority had been disregarded, he felt that the good of the Church required recognition of the validity of the agreement since it had been signed in the name of the Church.

De Baranda's attitude can be favourably contrasted with that of Cardinal Glemp.

Analysis

The Weltanschauung *of Cardinal Glemp*

The personalities of Cardinal Glemp, Cardinal Macharski and others clearly played an important role in the development of the controversy. One can only speculate as to the reasons for certain pronouncements and actions by the people involved. Cardinal Glemp has often been accused of anti-semitism, which he has always vigorously denied. It is very difficult to assess the validity of such accusations since a variety of attitudes are often covered by the term 'anti-semitic'. It is more appropriate, therefore, to concentrate on more tangible features of the Primate's behaviour and his *Weltanschauung*.

Many of the accusations are clearly oversimplifications. How many critics of Cardinal Glemp were aware, for example, that he visited the Warsaw Synagogue in 1983 or that it was he who started the unofficial commemorations of the fortieth anniversary of the Warsaw Ghetto Uprising in 1983? On *Yom ha-Shoah* on 10 April that year, Cardinal Glemp celebrated a special mass in the Church of St Augustine which is located within the area of the former Warsaw ghetto. During the mass he delivered a homily devoted to the Jewish martyrdom. The unofficial celebrations were organised independently of the Polish government by the opposition because most Poles, including Jewish Poles, refused to commemorate the event together with the then military rulers of the country. Marek Edelman, the last surviving commander of the uprising, felt that the Jews had fought for human dignity and that the martial law imposed by General Jaruzelski was not compatible with this goal, so that to celebrate together with the government would betray the spirit of their struggle. Cardinal Glemp's homily was the first event in a long line of independent celebrations of the uprising.[4]

Furthermore, a careful reading of Cardinal Glemp's controversial homily at Jasna Góra monastery shows that he attempted to praise the Jews, and addressed them in terms of endearment, however clumsy. But many of the Cardinal's pronouncements showed extraordinary insensitivity and lack of judgement. These included controversial statements about the Polish opposition, the Germans, the Jews, and others. During the 200th anniversary celebrations of the French Revolution, the Primate decided to attend the celebrations in Puy-du-Fou devoted to the anti-revolutionary uprising in Vendée. Regardless of the rights or wrongs of the Catholic uprising, and of its bloody suppression by the revolutionary forces, and regardless of the negative aspects of the French revolution, it was particularly undiplomatic to celebrate in Vendée when the rest of the world commemorated the Revolution's ideals and achievements in Paris.

Another example of his ineptitude came during a public meeting in Brussels on 26 February 1987 when Cardinal Glemp was criticized for ignoring the Jewish victims of Auschwitz by describing the Polish Jews as Poles. He then replied 'The statement that 6 million Polish citizens perished during the Second World War does not exclude that there were also Jews among them; if you can calculate the number of people of Jewish descent among those Polish citizens it can be taken into account.' This statement which was reported in a Warsaw daily was greeted with incredulity by many Polish Catholics.[5] 46 Catholic and Jewish Poles, some of them prominent intellectuals, wrote an open letter of protest to the Primate asking for clarification, which never came.[6]

The words of the Jasna Góra homily were characteristic of a traditional and narrow Catholic outlook – typical of many pre-Vatican II churchmen. The Second Vatican Council changed considerably the official view about the role of the Jews in the Passion of Christ and about Catholic relations with the Jews and towards Judaism. These changes have been only slowly assimilated, especially among the older generation, and even among some members of the clergy. It is difficult to understand how a Cardinal could show so little understanding of the issue. This may be related to the Primate's political stance.

It is widely known that Cardinal Glemp is sympathetic towards the political thinking of Roman Dmowski and his National Democratic Party (1896–1919, later known under two different names). The party, which was traditionally anti-German rather than anti-Russian, believed in the nation-state and considered ethnic minorities to be a threat to the 'Polish element'. It supported 'organic work' (a practical, positivist approach to life opposed to the purely idealistic fight for independence), and was ready to cooperate with the authorities of the foreign partitioning powers in the 19th century until 1918. Cardinal Glemp, like the supporters of Dmowski, has often been accused of excessive pragmatism and *Realpolitik*.

Cardinal Glemp wrote a preface to a booklet, *Church, Nation and State*, containing reprinted parts of Dmowski's work. Dmowski was a clearly anti-semitic politician who considered the Jews to be an alien element. He blamed them for maintaining their separateness, even after formal assimilation, and accused them of corrupting European societies, even if that was not their intention:

The Nationalists then say: even if the Jews were angels morally, and geniuses mentally, even if they were of a superior species, the very fact of their existence among us and their close partici-pation in our life is fatal for our society and one has to get rid of them. (1933)[7]

Dmowski was not a sympathiser with the National Socialists in Germany and 'getting rid of the Jews' was not a euphemism for their extermination. He did, however, support mass Jewish emigration and economic boycott.

In his letter-preface the Primate wrote: 'Roman Dmowski was a politician, and political opinions have partisans and opponents. In the final outcome, truth wins. In Dmowski's writings, the idea of the connection between the Church and the Nation is truth, many times tested. In thanks for the re-edition of the ambitious thoughts of that great Pole I express the hope that they will serve to revive the Polish spirit and love for Poland.'[8]

The Cardinal was often criticised for his tolerance of openly anti-semitic activities at a church in Warsaw, such as the distribution of anti-semitic literature, including a Polish translation of *The Protocols of the Elders of Zion*. This ended only after considerable pressure from the independent Polish press and the intervention of the Anti-Defamation League. Many people were unhappy about his support for Maciej Giertych. Attacking the Primate, Krzysztof Wolicki writ-ing in *Kultura* suggested that he wished to control developments in Poland by creating a Catholic political party with strong nationalis-tic undertones.[9] Whether this is true or not, it is evident that he is a man of considerable ambition. He is well aware of the role the holders of his office have played in Poland. Between 1572 and 1795 a Primate was *interrex* – acting Head of State between the death of a king and election of his successor. The Primate has traditionally been more than just *primus inter pares*, first among the Bishops. Cardinal Glemp, lacking the charisma of his much-respected predecessor, Stefan Cardinal Wyszyński, has attempted to reassert his power over the Polish Church through his position.

The Cardinal has undoubtedly protected and fostered the interests of the Polish Church as he understood them. This was evident in his fight with the Communist government for permission to erect new churches, to excuse clerics from military service and to assert people's rights to religious education. These actions did not always coin-cide with the interests of the Catholic majority of the country, since they reflected the needs of the Church rather than those of the laity. This created a conflict with many believers and lower clergy. Some compared the Cardinal with his 19th-century predecessor Archbishop Count Ledóchowski who, despite being the Primate, was more interested in the Church than in Poland. For a long time Ledóchowski was regarded as a lackey of the Prussian government. This changed only with the *Kulturkampf*, when Bismarck challenged his prerogatives as a churchman, rather than as a Pole. Only then was he ready to challenge the Prussian government, and be banished to the Vatican. Cardinal Glemp wrote the preface to the recently published apologetic biography of Cardinal Ledóchowski.

Polish Criticism of the Primate

Criticism of the Primate also came from parts of the clergy. *Kronika Rzymska*, a periodical published by the Foundation of John Paul II in Rome, edited by monks and priests, printed an article commenting on the growing anti-clericalism in Poland. The author considered this to be the result of the conciliatory policy of the Church towards the Communist government. Polish society had lived through a severe political, social, and economic crisis between the years 1981 and 1989, whereas the clergy appeared to be living in relative opulence – by Polish standards. This was combined with the perception that many clergymen had abandoned the ideals of Solidarity which used to be those of the Church. People's wish to live in dignity was denied them by the Communist government with which some members of the Episcopate were seen to be compromising. Recalling the difficult days of Stalinism, the article pointed out that Stefan Cardinal Wyszyński himself tried to rescue the Church by negotiating and compromising with the authorities. His concessions, however, had a limit and he was ready at one stage to go to prison rather than to abandon his principles. 'This period appears to have been the most fruitful for him and for the whole Church, not only in Poland. The shepherd gave his life for his sheep. It is very bad if shepherds come to some arrangement with the wolves and pretend not to see how the wolves destroy the flock.' The author emphasised that the Church should always defend truth, justice, the rights of the persecuted and wronged. 'There is no doubt that one must talk, that one has to come to some agreement, but not at the price of credibility in the eyes of the faithful, of the persecuted, and of the whole nation.' Expressing strong disapproval and unease, the author concluded

> Transitory arrangements bring quiet, but they do not build
> peace. The Polish people are well aware on whom they can
> depend and whom they can trust. In difficult situations they
> always relied on the Church and trusted the Church. It is worrying that, as some say, many today are beginning to harbour
> doubts about the Church as the only guarantee of truth,
> freedom, identity and national independence.[10]

This voice was not an isolated one, but it was especially interesting considering its source. It has been noted many times that parts of the Polish Church hierarchy felt very uneasy about Solidarity and the opposition in general. Solidarity's emergence coincided with the nomination of Cardinal Glemp for the post of Primate, and with it the Church lost its unique role as the only official and large-scale independent force able to counter the Communists. The Church which had for years attempted to protect Polish society from the worst aspects of Communist rule found itself, especially between 1980 and 1981 and after 1988, just one among many political players. It lost its monopoly as the representative of the people.

This could not please a Primate so conscious of the past and present importance of the Episcopate. His often lukewarm support for Solidarity was widely noted, even abroad, as were his good relations with General Jaruzelski whom the Primate regarded as a 'true Pole who knows Polish history and literature well ... General Jaruzelski represents our country's interests and his government gains increasingly more appreciation on the practical level'.[11] In March 1987, when this interview was given, such appreciation of General Jaruzelski was shared (even according to confidential Communist opinion polls), by no more than 10–15 per cent of the population. The Primate was clearly out of step with the feelings of the majority. During his audience with the Pope, Jaruzelski is reported to have contrasted the patriotic spirit of the majority of Bishops and of Cardinal Glemp in particular with that of the priests who were fighting the government.

The Cardinal had difficulty in accepting the independence of the movement in general and of Wałęsa in particular, whom he considered would have made a 'good sacristan'. Glemp accused him of having been manipulated by extremists, an accusation levelled at all those who disagreed with the Primate. Neither Tadeusz

Mazowiecki, the Polish Prime Minister, nor Professor Bronisław Geremek, Chairman of the Solidarity Parliamentary Club, both of whom used to be chief advisors to Wałęsa, could be accused of extremism, although they are certainly independent. The open support given by the Primate to some anti-Solidarity candidates in the 1989 elections (all of whom lost) confirmed to many his political ambitions. The candidates he favoured were pro-Church, nationalistic, and right-wing. There has since been persistent talk that the Primate will attempt to form a Christian Democratic Party under his tutelage.

The Primate's general political outlook and his need to assert himself may have contributed to his lukewarm support for the Geneva agreement which, in his legalistic way, he regarded as merely a declaration, and not a commitment. As one highly critical commentator suggested, it might have suited his political goals to create an image of Polish Catholics under siege from alien Western forces. An 'anti-Polish conspiracy' could be used to rally many Catholics around the Primate who would then be able to create a mass Catholic party in support of his position. Cardinal Glemp fought for what he regarded as his privileges and was upset by the Vatican's intervention which he called a 'forcible' solution to the problem, rather than a 'positive' one. The intervention was probably seen by him as incompatible with the autonomous rights of national Churches granted by the Second Vatican Council. In the light of this the Pope's decision to intervene directly must be regarded as remarkable. It also partially explains the Pontiff's apparent reluctance to become openly involved in the controversy. As late as June 1989 he refused to discuss the matter with Jewish representatives of the Anti-Defamation League.

Another probable reason for Cardinal Glemp's reluctance to support the Geneva declaration was that he considered the issue to be of national importance and therefore in his domain as President of the Polish Episcopate and Primate. For this reason he was keen to assert his primacy over Cardinal Macharski, who as Archbishop of Cracow could be seen as his rival. Throughout his career Cardinal Glemp has found himself in the uncomfortable position of not being the most senior Polish churchman, or the one towards whom the devotion of most believers is directed. The election of a Polish Pope to the Vatican shifted the perception of where authority lay. Most Polish Catholics regard John Paul II as their Polish Pope and therefore Cardinal Glemp as only second-in-command. This is especially so because of the differing political attitudes of the two men. John Paul II was always seen as the protector of the vital interests of the Polish nation and the defender of the oppressed and politically persecuted. He was never regarded as a clergyman who would sacrifice the interests of his flock for that of the Church as an organisation. During and after the difficult period of martial law, the Polish population found much more comfort in the pronouncements of the Pope than in those of the Primate. Cardinal Glemp's personal popularity never equalled that of his predecessor who since his death has been referred to as the 'Primate of the Millenium'. This clearly raised difficulties for the Vatican which did not want to create a rift between itself and the Polish Primate. He in turn often attempted to assert his independence, which would have been easier had the Pontiff not known the local conditions so well and not been so popular in the country.

The Pope and the Cardinal

Many Jewish leaders had clearly distinguished between the line of the Primate and that of the Pope. A press release by Rabbi Leon Klenicki, Director of the Interfaith Affairs Department of the Anti-Defamation League, was significantly entitled 'Two Poles – Poles Apart'.[12]

Those Jews who deal with inter-religious relations and with the Vatican are well aware of the numerous pronouncements of the Pope on Jews and Judaism and are appreciative of them. As Rabbi Tanenbaum urged during the conference in Vienna in 1988, 'anyone who wishes to speak seriously about the role of the Pope in his inspired commitment to fostering genuine solidarity and mutual respect between the Catholic Church and the Jewish people has a moral duty to study the texts of his numerous addresses and declarations.'[13] He then proceeded to give a few examples of the Pope's thinking:

> The spiritual bond with Jews is properly understood as 'a sacred one; stemming as it does from the mysterious will of God'. The relationship is not marginal to the Church. It reaches to the very essence of the nature of Christian faith itself; so that to deny it is to deny something essential to the teaching of the Church.
>
> The dialogue between Catholics and Jews is not a dialogue between past (Judaism) and present (Christianity) realities; as if

the former had been 'superseded' or 'displaced' by the latter. 'On the contrary,' the Pope declared in his moving allocution to the Jewish community of Main, 'it is a question rather of reciprocal enlightenment and explanation, just as is the relationship between the Scriptures themselves'.

It could be said that ultimately the Jews and the present Pope have only two points of disagreement, first, the reluctance of the Vatican to establish diplomatic links with the state of Israel, and second, the Pope's insistence that Jerusalem should become an international city. The less informed criticise the Pope for granting two audiences to Arafat, and for claiming that the Catholics have a covenant with God, as mentioned earlier. Few Jews have noticed that the Pope has met right wing dictators (Pinochet), leaders of totalitarian countries (Gromyko, Jaruzelski), terrorists (Arafat), and morally dubious figures (Waldheim). The Holy See is not very discriminatory in granting audiences to official figures. Replying to criticism which denied the Pope the right to assert the chosenness of the Roman Catholic Church, Dr Sidney Brichto was dismayed, and stressed that both Jews and Catholics have a right to 'maintain their belief in the superiority of their own faith. Harmony must be achieved not by ignoring deep differences in perception between the two faiths, but by seeking a better understanding of them.'[14]

The Pope's attitude towards Israel is little understood. The Vatican does not see any doctrinal problems in recognising the state of Israel. However, the Curia is concerned about the fate of Christians in the Arab lands. In Israel and in the Lebanon there is a large Arab-Christian population and the Vatican takes their feelings into account. The Pope himself seems to be concerned about the fate of the Palestinian population in Israel and the Palestinian refugees elsewhere. He regards this primarily as a moral issue, although he clearly understands the political problems involved in solving the Palestinian question. As the Pope said in his apostolic letter *Redemptionis Anno*:

> For the Jewish people who live in the State of Israel and who preserve in that land such precious testimonies of their history and their faith, we must ask for the desired security and the due tranquillity that is the prerogative of every nation and condition of life and of progress for every society.

On 15 February 1985 in an audience with the American Jewish Committee commemorating the twentieth anniversary of *Nostra Aetate*, the Pope emphasised this point by saying:

I know also your concern for the peace and security of the Holy Land. May the Lord give to the land, and to all the peoples and nations in that part of the world, the blessings contained in the word *shalom*, so that, in the expression of the Psalmist, justice and peace may kiss.

It does not seem likely that the Pontiff would agree to recognise Israel with its present borders and with the Palestinians not having full civil and political rights. As far as Jerusalem is concerned, it appears that the Vatican would like to secure guarantees to preserve the sacred character of the city and grant equal status to all three monotheistic religions present there. The Israelis who regard Jerusalem as their capital have been ready to grant access to all holy places to Christians and Muslims but are not prepared to discuss the change of status of the city. Their record in granting this access is incomparably better than that of Jordan which ruled East Jerusalem, where these places are located, until 1967. Recently there have been Jewish attempts, some of them supported by members of the Israeli government, to change the precarious status quo in Jerusalem's Old City by violating the religious division of the quarters. This did not inspire confidence within the Vatican. The Pope, sympathetic as he may be towards Israel, is unlikely to abandon a policy which, for him, is based on moral principle.

Religious Differences

The conflict of course had a religious dimension. Judaism and Christianity have radical differences. The two-thousand-year history of relations between Christianity and Judaism also played a visible part. The very presence of a cross in Auschwitz was considered by many Jews to be a painful reminder of the role which the Catholic church played in their persecution. To some, the silent prayer of the Carmelites was a symbol of the Vatican's and of Pius XII's silence during the Holocaust. It was regarded as an attempt by the Catholics to expiate their past sins. Many saw the Nazis as Christians and blamed their atrocities on the Church's teachings. The Church itself admitted and accepted its faults and the inadequacy of its response to the Nazis, but did not regard them as Christian. This point was well understood by a famous Jewish poet, Joseph Brodsky:

I would like to stress that the word Jew is a racial term and Christian is a term describing religious allegiance. This means that a man who is a Jew is so above all for reasons of blood, and only secondly by reason of his faith, whereas a man becomes a Christian solely by reason of his faith.

In distinction to Jewish identity, which is acquired at the moment of birth, Christian identity comes when one follows the way of the Saviour, which the term itself suggests. It is not enough to be born, to be baptised and brought up in the spirit of the Church, for no faith is passed down by inheritance – it is always a question of personal choice and behaviour. In a word, a man becomes a Christian through his deeds, and not through his words.

The Jews murdered in Auschwitz were not murdered by Christians who regarded themselves as Christians, but by Germans who regarded themselves as Christians and lost their right to do so the moment they committed the first murder. A Jew ceases to be a Jew only at the moment of death; a Christian can easily perish long before his physical death. What happened in Auschwitz was the triumph of the bestial in man, and not at all a religious drama.

John Paul II often talked about 'the spiritual heritage of Israel for the Church', and of 'common spiritual patrimony' which he saw as valid not only in the past but in the present. The Church has not always shared this view. In part, the reaction of the Jewish community was the result of deep resentment against the role played by Pope Pius XII during the war and, specifically in the Polish context, at the attitude of the Polish Church hierarchy in the inter-war period. Pius XII was frequently criticised for not openly condemning the extermination of the Jews, although it is now known that he did undertake diplomatic action on their behalf. Some Catholics still maintain that the Pope's open condemnation would not have saved the Jews, but would rather have endangered Jewish converts to Christianity (some of whom were left in peace) and unleashed large scale persecution of the Church. This judgement is not shared by the Jews and by many Polish Catholics whose Church was very severely affected by Nazi policies. During the Second World War the Nazis killed 1,932 priests, including six bishops, 850 monks, and 289 nuns. Some dioceses lost half of their clergy, apart from the substantial destruction of churches. Thousands of clergymen were affected by the terror and many were sent to concentration camps. In view of this, the Polish population and the government in exile based in London could not comprehend the policy of the Vatican and frequently appealed for an unequivocal condemnation.

The Polish Catholic Church between the wars had a largely nationalistic outlook. Catholic papers like *Mały Dziennik*, *Głos Narodu*, *Rycerz Niepokalanej*, or *Samoobrona Narodu* took a distinctly anti-communist but also an anti-liberal and xenophobic line. A more tolerant trend in Polish Catholicism was represented by the periodical *Verbum* and centres at Laski near Warsaw or around *Odrodzenie* – the association of Catholic University Students. The latter, however, were always in a minority. Since the Church equated Catholicism with Polishness, Jews were somehow not fully Polish. In the eyes of the clergy they were often associated with left-wing politics, free-thinking liberalism, socialism, or even communism and freemasonry. The separation of church and state was rejected by the clergy and by many lay Catholics, since Poland was considered to be a bastion of Roman Catholicism fighting the atheistic barbarians from the east. Generally speaking, the hierarchy and the religious papers were against the persecution of the Jews, but were tolerant of segregation (such as the ghetto benches) and of economic boycott.

Some positions taken by the hierarchy, however, were ambiguous. In 1936 the Primate, August Hlond, issued a pastoral letter in which he criticised various aspects of public life. He perceived as the biggest threats to society godlessness and hatred:

> Apart from godlessness the greatest monstrosity of our relations is making hatred a slogan, principle and duty ... Here hatred has spread particularly in public life. He who belongs to a different camp, and particularly if he is a political opponent, is seen as the enemy.

In this context the Primate spoke out against the Jews:

> They oppose the Catholic Church, they are steeped in freethinking, they consitute an avantgarde of godlessness, bolshevism and subversive activity. It is a fact that they exert a pernicious influence on public morality and that their publishing houses are spreading pornography. It is true that Jews are swindlers, usurers, and that they are engaged in fostering immoral earnings. It is true that the effect of the Jewish youth upon the Catholic is – in the religious and ethical sense – negative. But we

must not be unjust. This does not apply to all Jews. There are very many Jews who are believers, honest, righteous, merciful, doing good works. The family life of many Jews is healthy and edifying. And there are among Jews people morally quite outstanding, noble and honorable people. I must warn against an ethical attitude imported from abroad. It contradicts Catholic ethics. One is permitted to love one's own nation more, one is forbidden to hate anyone. Including the Jews ... It is not permitted to attach Jews, to beat them, to cripple them, to blacken them. In the Jew, too, one should respect the human being and neighbour, even if one is unable to respect the indescribable tragedy of this nation which was the guardian of the messianic idea and which gave birth to the Saviour. For when God's grace enlightens the Jew, and when he sincerely approaches his and our Messiah, let us greet him joyfully into the Christian ranks.[16]

This pronouncement of the Primate, while supporting the traditional Catholic view of the Jews, also constituted an important attempt to condemn politically motivated assaults on the Jewish community and warned against acceptance of fascist propaganda emanating from Germany. Most other bishops shared this outlook in the 1930s. The inter-war years were characterised by political struggle between the nationalistic right-wing and Christian democratic groups supporting Poland as a Catholic nation state, and the socialist or liberal lay intelligentsia and some peasants who were strongly anti-clerical. The conspiracy theory which was very much present in the Church's thinking encouraged the idea of imminent danger to Poland coming from Bolshevik, freemason, or Jewish circles. Cardinal Hlond and his bishops regarded the lay intelligentsia as a group who were 'swarming with the errors of the 19th century, with materialistic doctrinairianism, with false views on religion and morality, with disastrous social and political principles.' This view did little to encourage liberalism and tolerance in Polish society.

During the war, the Church, which was severely persecuted by the Nazis, did not issue any pronouncements about the Jews. Despite pre-war prejudices, the Church's record during the Nazi occupation was excellent. The clergy suffered together with the rest of society and showed great solidarity with it. The clergy were also very active in helping to save the Jews. There are no accurate records available but at a rough estimate several thousand Jews, particularly children, were saved by religious orders and orphanages. For example, Matylda Getter, the Provincial of the Franciscan Sisters of the Family of Mary, in collaboration with practically all the houses of the order, helped well over 1000 Jews.[17]

Even some anti-semitic priests, such as Father Marceli Godlewski, who was linked with the National Democratic Party before the war, ended up sheltering Warsaw Jews. The most astounding case is undoubtedly that of Father Stanisław Trzeciak, the author of many virulently anti-semitic pamphlets and the personification of the most intransigent form of Polish anti-semitism before the war. During the war he supported the nuns of the Order of the Immaculate Conception in their efforts to hide Jewish girls in their Catholic boarding school.[18] Regardless of the prejudiced views of many Catholics, it was a Catholic organisation, *Front Odrodzenia Polski*, which initiated organised help for the Jews and later became the Council for Aid to Jews, Żegota. So the record of the Polish Church towards the Jews was very mixed.

After the war, the bishops perceived persecution of the Jews largely in political terms. They faced a cruel dilemma – how to defend the Jews against the violence to which they were exposed without, at the same time, supporting the Communist authorities, amongst whom the Jewish presence was highly visible. The government openly accused Poles of anti-semitism and represented itself as the only defender of the Jews. As Krystyna Kersten pointed out, the stereotypes of a Pole Catholic and of Judeo-Communism were strengthened by the policy of the government.[19] It was no coincidence that official posters praising the courageous fighters of the Warsaw Ghetto could be found side by side with others condemning the 'dribbling reactionary dwarves' of the Home Army. The public began to associate the Jews with the worst attacks against the most patriotic sections of Polish society. The Church by and large stopped condemning the Jews for religious reasons and condemned them for political ones instead.

Attacks against the Jews were not supported by the Church. In January 1946, Cardinal Hlond told Professor Michał Zylberg, a representative of the Jewish Religious Associations, that the attacks

> Fill me with real sadness. Without repeating arguments arising from Christian principles, in Poland there are no objective reasons for the spread of anti-semitism. This is madness on the part of those who are still conspiring, remaining in the forests.

They think they are participating in politics, that by attacking Jews they are fighting the government. I condemn their activities as a Catholic and as a Pole.[20]

After the Kiecle pogrom in July 1946 during which 42 Jews were killed similar attempts were made elsewhere. Thus in Częstochowa, Bishop Kubina, who in 1936 divided the world into the followers of Christ and of Anti-Christ, the latter being 'the materialistic capitalists and communists who have embraced the Jewish battle-cry: "we do not want Christ to rule over us"' prevented a pogrom in his town by issuing a public appeal:

All statements about the ritual murder are lies. No one from the Christian community either in Kielce or in Częstochowa or anywhere else in Poland has been injured by the Jews for religious and ritual purposes.[21]

At the same time, the Primate and the Episcopate shared the perception of the majority of the Poles when they stated:

The fact that conditions are deteriorating should be blamed to a large extent on the Jews who today occupy leading roles in Polish government and attempt to introduce a structure of government which the majority of the nation does not desire ... In the fatal armed struggles, in the fighting on the political frontline in Poland it is regrettable that some Jews lose their lives, but a disproportionately larger number of Poles lose their lives.[22]

According to some estimates up to 2,000 Jews lost their lives in the first post-war years, although it is impossible to say how many of them were killed as Jews and how many as communists. These first years witnessed the most brutal repression by the new regime of the hostile population. By October 1944, 100,000 Poles had already found themselves imprisoned by the Communists and thousands were killed. In desperation, many of those who had fought the Nazis refused to lay down arms and used them to kill Communists and Jews, regardless of the political affiliation of the latter. Commenting on this phenomenon, Abel Kainer wrote in 1983 in the underground quarterly *Krytyka*:

The Jews had something to fear then. But their behaviour only served to confirm the anti-semites, who were organised in groups, of the righteousness of their struggle against the Jews, and converted God knows how many others to their point of view. This, in turn, made the Jews even more dependent on the Communists.[23]

Effect of Religious Differences on the Convent Controversy

Other problems were related to Catholic concepts such as the communion of saints, repentance, penance, expiation, and forgiveness. The Jewish community thought that the Carmelites, by their presence in Auschwitz, were attempting to force them to recognise the validity of these. The very fact that the nuns were praying for the victims and for the souls of the perpetrators was interpreted as an equivocal act of forgiveness. The Christian Church is based on love and forgiveness while Judaism stresses justice. As Simon Dubnow pointed out in his critique of the Russian philosopher, Solovyev, who advocated national altruism and universalism according to which one should 'love all the nations as your own':

> The difference of opinion between the 'Christian philosopher' Solovyev and myself reveals once more the difference between national outlooks on life. It is the old controversy between *love*, the subjective principle of the Gospels, and the objective standard of *justice* embedded in the Jewish ethical tradition. Judaism never set up ethical postulates which were incapable of realization. It never built systems which were 'not of this world.' It formulated ideals which could be reached and hence demanded with all the severity of the law that they be carried out ...[24]

The Jews found it offensive that the nuns were praying for the murdered and their murderers alike. The fact that they wished to pray for the Jewish victims as well only compounded the offence. The Catholics can forgive even if they do not forget – for the Jews, only God can forgive.

The Catholics found it perfectly natural to pray at Auschwitz which, through the martyrdom of thousands of Catholics, has become a sacred place. Clifford Longley explained this difference in a sensitive article:

> The Jewish instinct in a place like that is to leave it as desolate as possible, physically, morally and philosophically. Auschwitz is

not sacred to the Jews; it is the very opposite of sacred. To extract solace or meaning from such things, let alone find holiness there, is to try to mitigate the evil, to pretend it was somehow not as bad as it really was, and thus to belittle the millions who died there.

But the Christian instinct is the exact reverse; it is to sanctify such a place. Christians consecrate their cemeteries, build shrines where accidents or executions happen, celebrate their martyrs and call the place of martyrdom holy. There is also a convent of nuns on the site of the gallows at Tyburn, praying for peace and for the dead.[25]

Few Jews shared the feelings of Alma Perepletnik who did not object to Catholic prayer at the camp, explaining:

My parents were Jews who perished in Auschwitz. The last postcard they sent from the camp at Drancy before deportation was addressed to a nun. It included the words: 'Pray for us'.[26]

Simple misunderstandings made matters worse as the horrified reaction to the phrase 'conversion of strayed brothers' used in the original appeal for funds to build a Carmel testified. Catholics cannot convert anybody after death but most Jews have little understanding of the complexity of Catholic doctrine.

The presence of a cross at the convent in Auschwitz offended the Jews who argued that there must not be a cross in a Jewish cemetery. This was linked to the interpretation of Auschwitz-Birkenau as the largest Jewish cemetery in history. But from the strictly religious point of view, this is far from self-evident. What is Auschwitz for religious Jews? Is it a cemetery? Is it a museum-monument? Or is it the site of a massacre? There are certain rules in Jewish law which would suggest that Auschwitz could not be regarded as a cemetery, but rather the place of a massacre, or even as a category *sui generis*. The Jews object to the presence of a convent and have repeatedly rejected the suggestion that they could build a synagogue there as unacceptable under Jewish law. This may be an issue of taxonomy and terminology. It is possible for the Jews to have a funeral chapel (*ohel*) at a cemetery. These considerations notwithstanding, it is obvious that the majority of the Jewish community profoundly disagreed with a permanent Catholic religious presence in a place where millions of Jews perished.

Analysis

The Museum in Auschwitz

A seemingly separate issue but one which is linked with that of the Carmel is that of the museum in Auschwitz. The museum covers a vast area (195 hectares) and includes both Auschwitz I and Auschwitz II (Birkenau) although exhibitions are to be found exclusively in the former. Birkenau has been left mainly intact while Auschwitz is surrounded by a lively town of over 40,000 inhabitants, and is itself very much a major tourist attraction complete with kiosks, a self-service canteen etc. Since 1946 the camp has been visited by 20 million people, 20 per cent of whom were from abroad. Approximately 700,000 people pass through Auschwitz every year. The sheer scale of the camp-museum poses enormous logistical problems as it is not easy to show the complex to so many people. The large number of tourists also poses a moral problem: how to educate the general public in a way which is sensitive to, and respectful of, the millions who perished there.[27] It is not surprising that in 1986 there were Polish Jews who felt that the conflict over the convent was less relevant than solving the problem of the museum. A zone of silence was proposed and a limit to the number of organised tours and accompanying trade.

Many doubts have also been raised about the way the museum is organised. Of 28 'barracks' or 'blocks', five are used for a general exhibition and the others are devoted to so-called 'national exhibitions' organised by the states whose citizens were prisoners of Auschwitz. The exception is the Jewish block which is devoted to 'the martyrology and struggle of the Jews' which was created by the Poles rather than by the Israelis. The blocks also contain offices, research centres, a film room, etc. The main function of the museum was to create an archive for all documents related to Auschwitz-Birkenau, to preserve the camps in their original state together with objects found there, to conduct and publish research, and to educate the general public. The objects preserved include 79 cubic metres of shoes, irons, cutlery; 2,479 kilograms of glasses, razors, buttons; 3,500 suitcases, 29,000 toothbrushes, 460 prosthetic limbs, and thousands of other objects.

The museum employs almost 200 people including 120 guides who enable it to remain open all year.

The main problem with the exhibitions is that they were created largely in the early 1950s, and have not changed substantially since. Although the museum was the initiative of former prisoners, its organisation was restricted by the political principles of Stalinist Poland. As such the museum was to be devoted to the 'martyrdom of the Polish and other nations' at the hands of the fascists. Fascism was considered to be the final and most brutal stage of 'monopoly capitalism' and was the 'logical outcome' of the contradictions inherent in capitalist society. All struggle against Nazism was portrayed as a part of the class war fought and won by the 'progressive forces of history' against the imperialist militant monopoly capitalists. In this spirit of internationalism, it was not considered to be appropriate to mention distinct national experiences. Those who had opposed the Nazis, but who were not Communists, were scarcely mentioned.

A separate Jewish block was not opened until 1978. Those blocks opened by other Communist states in the 1960s and 1970s described the fate of their citizens sent to Auschwitz without discussing the singular treatment accorded to the Jews from their countries. The nature of the *Shoah* was therefore distorted by an attempt to 'de-Judeaise' it. A visitor to the Auschwitz museum would not be made aware that the Jews were the main victims of the camp. The information about how many Jews were murdered there is nowhere to be found. The partial 'Polonisation' of the Holocaust has already been discussed. The Communist national pavilions in many ways followed the same pattern, although the one organised by the Bulgarians in 1977 was totally devoted to the history of Communism in their country and did not mention Auschwitz at all.

For the Poles, the large number of Catholics killed in Auschwitz made it easier to create an area which concentrated entirely on their fate. The cell of Father Kolbe is commemorated by a plaque. The 'Wall of Death' where thousands of Gentiles were shot, a seven-metre-high cross on the site of early executions and the Carmelite Convent are all in close proximity to each other. As a result, this part of the museum became for Poles a sacred place of Christian martyrdom. As Jean-Charles Szurek remarked, 'the old anti-fascist and Polish memory' of the camp was replaced by 'a new Catholic and still Polish memory'.

The problem of the museum, which for many Jews and Poles was ultimately of far greater importance than the Carmelite presence on the site, will soon be resolved. In the autumn of 1989 Tadeusz Mazowiecki established a commission to consider the future of the museum at Auschwitz, the secretary of which is Stefan Wilkanowicz, and which includes as one of its members Stanisław Krajewski. In May 1990 the commission members met at Yarnton

Manor in Oxford with a group of Jewish intellectuals and agreed on the principles which were to guide the reorganisation of the museum. There is little doubt that, given the favourable attitude both of the new Polish government and those serving on the committee, the Auschwitz-Birkenau complex will in time be transformed into a museum acceptable to all concerned.

Conclusions

The main reason for the outbreak of the controversy about the Carmelite Convent in Auschwitz was an almost total lack of understanding of Jewish matters on the part of the Poles. Polish knowledge of Judaism was with few exceptions non-existent. The Convent was located on the site of the concentration/extermination camp Auschwitz-Birkenau because the well-meaning nuns wanted to pray for its victims. No one in Poland understood that this gesture would be offensive to both religious and secular Jews. The conflict was exacerbated by the lack of historical knowledge on the part of both communities. There was also the problem of a deep rift in the mutual perception of both history and religion. The difficulties in resolving the conflict were attributable largely to the symbolic nature of Auschwitz. It was a fight between two different symbols – of Jewish and Polish martyrdom.

Both communities used their respective interpretation of the significance of Auschwitz to strengthen their national identities. Each interpretation threatened the identity of the other. There were people in both communities who understood this problem but the majority ignored it for too long. The conflict became difficult to solve because reason was no match for the power of symbols.

The Jewish community was, on the whole, only marginally better informed about Christianity than Christians about Judaism. The problems intensified because of misunderstandings about Christian concepts and the organisation of the Church. The Jews knew little about the ways in which the Catholic Church was organised and how it functioned. They also had little understanding of the significant role it played in contemporary Polish history, during which it was a source of hope and support for ordinary people struggling first with the Nazi, and then with the Soviet tyranny.

The controversy was intensified by the fact that it affected Jewish and Church politics. The world Jewish community is pluralistic, and as such is represented by a variety of organisations competing for the right to speak for all Jews. This situation both enables and encourages small and extreme groups to make spectacular gestures and to claim that they defend Jewish interests 'better' than more moderate ones. The controversy provoked open disagreement amongst Church officials in which the competence of a number of clergymen was questioned. Those whose pride had been wounded were not averse to putting obstacles in the way of a quick and amicable settlement. The traditional divisions between liberal and nationalistic Polish Catholics, which had existed since the 19th century, were brought into the open by the controversy. There was a clear distinction between the line taken by the Pope and many lay Catholics, and that adopted by the Primate.

The adverse effects of the controversy on Christian-Jewish relations were quite serious. The links established after the Second Vatican Council were put under severe strain. This was especially apparent amongst Catholics and Jews not directly involved in inter-religious affairs, although it affected their official representatives as well. Surprisingly, given its Polish context, the conflict had very little effect on actual Polish-Jewish relations. Undoubtedly it strengthened mutual prejudices which have long existed in both communities. At the same time, Polish-Jewish dialogue continued unabated. Polish and Jewish organisations in the United States, Canada, and Great Britain issued joint statements about the affair. The joint appeals of the National Polish-American Jewish-American Council, the Polish American Congress, the American Jewish Committee, the Federation of Poles in Great Britain, the 1945 Holocaust Survival Society, the Canadian Polish Congress, and other organisations were distributed and published in various newspapers. The Institute for Polish-Jewish Studies in Oxford, which for many years, has, through its high standards, set an example to both communities as to how to conduct debate on controversial issues, also helped to resolve the Auschwitz conflict. Its President Antony Polonsky, always a voice of moderation, was instrumental in bringing it to an end. Finally this unseemly row which besmirched the memory of the millions of Auschwitz-Birkenau victims demonstrated that, despite the efforts of extremists, moderate counsels could and would prevail. By the end of 1991, the Carmelite Convent will have been moved from the old theatre in Auschwitz.

NOTES

CHAPTER 1

1 See A. Ciechanowiecki, 'A footnote to the history of the integration of converts into the ranks of the *szlachta* in the Polish Lithuanian Commonwealth', *The Jews in Poland* ed. C. Abramsky et. al. (Oxford: Basil Blackwell, 1986), pp. 64–9.

2 M. J. Rosman, 'A Minority Views the Majority: Jewish Attitudes Towards the Polish Lithuanian Commonwealth and Interaction with Poles', in *POLIN: A Journal of Polish-Jewish Studies*, vol. 4, 1989 (Oxford: Basil Blackwell), pp. 31–41.

3 E. Mendelsohn, *The Jews of East Central Europe Between the World Wars* (Bloomington: Indiana University Press, 1983), pp. 25–8.

4 E. Mendelsohn, 'Interwar Poland: good for the Jews or bad for the Jews?', in Abramsky et. al., op. cit., pp. 138–9.

CHAPTER 2

1 A. Montague, 'The Carmelite Convent at Auscwitz: A Documentary Survey', *IJA Research Report* (London), No. 8, October 1987, p. 2.

2 Ibid.

3 Ibid., p. 6.

4 W. Bartoszewski, 'Polish-Jewish Relations in occupied Poland, 1939–1945', in Abramsky et al., op. cit., p. 150.

5 D. Czech, 'Most important events in the history of the Concentration Camp Auschwitz-Birkenau', in *From the History of KL Auschwitz, Auschwitz Museum*, (Poland, 1967).

6 P. Vidal-Naquet, 'Auschwitz: de la réalité aux symboles', *Regards* (Brussels), No. 171, 1986.

7 P. Vidal-Naquet, *Les assasins de la mémoire* (Paris: La Découverte, 1987), p. 77.

8 Y. Bauer, 'Fighting the distortions', in *Jerusalem Post*, 22 September 1989.

9 P. Vidal-Naquet, 'Auschwitz ...', op. cit.

10 Publishers' insert to vol. XI, *Wielka Encyklopedia Powszechna PWN* (Warsaw: PWN, 1968).

11 M. Gilbert, *The Holocaust: The Jewish Tragedy* (London: Collins, 1986), pp. 287, 853n.

12 A. Steg, 'La spécificité d'Auschwitz', in *Regards* (Brussels), No. 175, 1987.

13 I. Irwin-Zarecka, *Neutralizing Memory: The Jew in Contemporary Poland* (New Brunswick: Transaction Books, 1988).

14 E. Berberyusz, 'Guilt by Neglect', in *My Brother's Keeper*, ed. A. Polonsky (London: Routledge, 1990), pp. 69–71.

15 A. Smolar, 'Jews as a Polish problem', *Daedelus*, spring 1987, p. 50.

16 P. Korzec, J-C. Szurek, 'Jews and Poles under Soviet Occupation (1939–1941): Conflicting Interests', in *POLIN* vol. 4, op. cit., pp. 204–25.

17 I. Grudzinska-Gross and J.T. Gross (eds), *War Through Children's Eyes* (Stanford: Hoover Institution Press, 1981).

18 Quoted in Smolar, op. cit., p. 39.

19 A. Smolar, 'Tabu i niewinność', *Aneks* (London) 41–42, 1986, p. 98. This is the Polish version of the article in *Daedelus* (fn. 15). My translation differs from the American version.
20 W. Bartoszewski, 'The Founding of the All-Polish Anti-Racist League in 1946', *POLIN* vol. 4, op. cit., pp. 243–54.
21 W. Bartoszewski in 'Ethical Problems of the Holocaust in Poland', in Polonsky op. cit., pp. 227–8.
22 W. Siła-Nowicki, 'A Reply to Jan Błoński' in Polonsky op. cit., p. 67.
23 T. Prekerowa, 'The "Just" and the "Passive"', in Polonsky op. cit., pp. 72–80.
24 J. Garliński, 'The Underground Movement in Auschwitz Concentration Camp', *POLIN* vol. 1, 1986, pp. 212–26.
25 J. Karski, 'Shoah (Zatlada)', *Kultura* (Paris), No. 11 1985, p. 124.
26 Z. Kałużyński, 'Odmawiam Przebaczenia', *Polityka* (Warsaw), 7 December 1985.
27 Jerzy Turowicz, '"Shoah" w polskich oczach', *Tygodnik Powszechny*, 10 November 1985.
28 C. Lanzmann speaking in Oxford on 23 September 1985.
29 Y. Gutman, 'Polish and Jewish historiography on the question of Polish-Jewish relations during World War II', in Abramsky op. cit., pp. 182, 183.
30 L. Goldberger (ed.), *The Rescue of the Danish Jews* (New York and London: New York University Press, 1987).
31 Interview with Simon Wiesenthal, Radio Free Europe (Munich), 7 January 1989.

CHAPTER 3

1 Montague, op. cit.. p. 5 ff.
2 Discalced or 'barefoot' Carmelites, a stricter branch of the order, reformed by St Teresa of Avila in the 16th century.
3 Cardinal Macharski, 'Znak nadziei w Oświęcimiu', *Tygodnik Powszechny*, 2 March 1986.
4 Montague, op. cit., p. 8.
5 Ibid.
6 Montague, op. cit., p. 9.
7 Montague, op. cit., p. 10.
8 Quoted from I. Filarski, *L'affaire du Carmel d'Auschwitz – Contribution a l'étude des relations judéo-polonaises. Etude de cas*, unpublished thesis, Institut d'Etudes Politiques de Paris, 1988, p. 12.
9 Ibid.
10 Ibid., pp. 15–16.
11 S. Krajewski, 'Auschwitz, klasztor i Żydzi', *Tygodnik Powszechny*, 22 June 1986.
12 J. Turowicz, 'Karmel w Oświęcimiu', *Tygodnik Powszechny*, 22 June 1986.

CHAPTER 4

1 Reprinted in *Christian Jewish Relations*, No. 3, September 1986, pp. 47–51.
2 Rabbi Norman Solomon, ibid., pp. 42–6.
3 *Regards* (Brussels), No. 171, 1986.
4 Montague, op. cit., p. 18.
5 Ibid.
6 Reprinted in *Christian Jewish Relations*, No. 2, summer 1987, pp. 53–5.
7 Montague, op. cit., p. 19.
8 Reprinted in *L'Osservatore Romano* (Polish edition), No. 10/11, 1989.
9 Fr S. Musiał, 'II spotkanie w Genewie', *Tygodnik Powszechny*, 15 March 1987.

CHAPTER 5

1 W. Siła-Nowicki, 'A reply to Jan Błoński', Polonsky op. cit., pp. 59–68.
2 A full account of the debate can be found in Polonsky op. cit.

CHAPTER 6

1 The Rev. John T. Pawlikowski, OSM, 'Recent Controversies over the Auschwitz Convent and "Shoah"', paper delivered at a meeting of the Polish American Historical Association, Washington, DC, 28 December 1987.
2 I. Filarski, 'L'Affaire du Carmel D'Auschwitz', *L'Autre Europe*, No. 20, 1989, p. 182.
3 Ibid., p. 183.
4 Ibid., p. 185.
5 Jewish Telegraphic Agency, 23 December 1988.
6 Ibid., 2 February 1989.
7 Ibid.
8 *L'Osservatore Romano* (Polish edition), No. 10/11, 1989.
9 Ibid.
10 Ibid.
11 *The Jewish Chronicle*, 3 March 1989.
12 Ibid.
13 Ibid., 22 February 1989.
14 *Jewish Chronicle*, 3 March 1989.
15 Jewish Telegraphic Agency, 24 February 1989.
16 *Jewish Chronicle*, 3 March 1989.
17 Ibid., 24 March 1989.
18 Ibid., 12 May 1989.
19 Jewish Telegraphic Agency, 28 March 1989.
20 Reuter, Tel Aviv, 13 April 1989.
21 *Times*, letter dated 29 April 1989.
22 Jewish Telegraphic Agency, 5 May 1989.
23 *Forward*, 19 May 1989.
24 Jewish Telegraphic Agency, 31 May 1989.
25 Ibid., 8 June 1989.
26 Ibid.
27 *Aneks* (London), No. 53, 1989, pp. 137–9.
28 *Tygodnik Powszechny*, 27 May 1990.
29 *Życie Warszawy*, 21 June 1989.
30 *Jewish Chronicle*, 23 June 1989.
31 A. Kainer, 'Solidarity and Martial Law: The Jewish Dimension', *Studium Papers* (Ann Arbor, Michigan), No. 2, April, 1989 p. 56.
32 *Jewish Chronicle*, 14 July 1989.

CHAPTER 7

1 *Życie Warszawy*, 18 July 1989.
2 *Independent*, 18 July 1989.
3 *Gazeta Wyborcza*, 17 July 1989.
4 *Życie Warszawy*, 20 July 1989.
5 *International Herald Tribune*, 29 August 1989.
6 *WAI*, No. 12, 26 July 1989.
7 *Observer*, 23 July 1989.
8 *Daily Telegraph*, 27 July 1989.
9 *Jewish Chronicle*, 28 July 1989.

10 Ibid., 11 August 1989.
11 Ibid.
12 Ibid., 25 August 1989.
13 Ibid.
14 Ibid.
15 *Times*, 1 September 1989.
16 *Jewish Chronicle*, August 1989.
17 Pawlikowski, op. cit.
18 *Regards*, No. 171, 1986, p. 28.
19 *Znak*, No. 347, 1983, p. 167.

CHAPTER 8

1 *Jewish Chronicle*, 25 August 1989.
2 *Życie Warszawy*, 15 August 1989.
3 Ibid.
4 *Jewish Chronicle*, 25 August 1989.
5 Ibid.
6 K. Adler, 'Controversy over the Carmelite Convent at Auschwitz 1988–89', *IJA Research Report*, No. 7, 1989.
7 Ibid.
8 *Polityka*, 26 August 1989.
9 *Życie Warszawy*, 25 August 1989.
10 Adler, op. cit.
11 Reuter (Warsaw), 31 August 1989.
12 Ibid.
13 *La Republica*, 2 September 1989.
14 Jewish Telegraphic Agency, 30 August 1989.
15 *Jewish Chronicle*, 8 September 1989.
16 Ibid.
17 Jewish Telegraphic Agency, 30 August 1989.
18 Ibid.
19 Ibid.
20 Ibid.
21 *Le Monde*, 29 August 1989.
22 *Jewish Chronicle*, 1 September 1989.
23 Ibid.
24 *Jewish Chronicle*, September 1989.
25 *Independent*, 11 September 1989.
26 Ibid., 12 September 1989.
27 PAP, 11 September 1989.
28 *Jewish Chronicle*, 8 September 1989.
29 *Times*, 21 August 1989.
30 *Evening Standard*, 7 September 1989.
31 Ibid., 13 September 1989.
32 *Jewish Chronicle*, 22 September 1989.
33 *L'Osservatore Romano* (Polish edition), No. 10/11, 1989.
34 *Le Monde*, 12 September 1989.
35 *Sunday Telegraph*, 17 September 1989.
36 *Sunday Times*, 17 September 1989.
37 *Gazeta Wyborcza*, 16 October 1989.
38 *Jewish Chronicle*, 15 September 1989.

Notes

CHAPTER 9

1 *Independent*, 20 September 1989.
2 *International Herald Tribune*, 26 September 1989.
3 *Times*, 21 September 1989.
4 *International Herald Tribune*, 22 September 1989.
5 Ibid.
6 *Kultura* (Paris), October 1989.
7 'Jews and Christians in a Pluralistic World', conference organized by the *Institut für die Wissenschaften vom Menschen*, Vienna, 27–30 November, 1988.
8 *The Jewish Week*, 24 November 1989, p. 32.
9 Report of Sir Sigmund Sternberg's and Antony Polonsky's visit to Poland, 24–28 November 1989.

CHAPTER 10

1 Montague, op. cit., p. 9.
2 A. Fandrejewska, 'Konflikt w Oświęcimiu: z pierwszych stron gazet trafit pod furtę klasztorną', *Polityka*, 29 July 1989.
3 *L'Osservatore Romano* (Polish edition), No. 10/11, 1989.
4 Kainer, op. cit., p. 57.
5 *Życie Warszawy*, 26 February 1987.
6 *Kultura* (Paris), September 1987.
7 J. Kłoczowski, L. Mullerowa, and J. Skarbek, *Zarys dziejów Kościoła katolickiego w Polsce*, (Krakow: Znak, 1986), p. 304.
8 K. Gebert, 'Dialogue and Discord', *Studium Papers* (Ann Arbor, Michigan), No. 2, April 1989, p. 65.
9 *Kultura* (Paris), October 1989.
10 op. cit., March 1988, pp. 126–8.
11 Ibid., April 1987.
12 Anti Defamation League press release, autumn 1989.
13 Rabbi Mark Tanenbaum, 'Jewish-Christian Relations: Achievements and Unfinished Agendas', paper delivered at the IWM conference in Vienna, November 1988.
14 Minutes of a meeting of the Israel Diaspora Trust of 5 October 1989.
15 J. Brodsky, *International Herald Tribune*, 7 September 1989.
16 A. Smolar, 'Jews as a Polish Problem', op. cit., pp. 51–2; Kłoczowski et al., op. cit., pp. 306–7.
17 J. Kłoczowski, 'The Religious Orders and the Jews in Nazi-Occupied Poland', POLIN vol. 3, op. cit., p. 241.
18 W. Bartoszewski, and Z. Lewin (eds)., *Righteous Among Nations* (London: Earlscourt Publications, 1969), p. 361.
19 K. Kersten, *Narodziny Systemu Władzy* (Paris: Libella, 1986).
20 Ibid., p. 170.
21 R. Modras, 'The Catholic Church and Antisemitism in Poland: 1933–1939', seminar report, Annenberg Institute, Philadelphia, 12 October 1989.
22 Kersten, op. cit.
23 A. Kainer, 'Żydzi a komunizm', *Krytyka*, No. 15, 1983, p. 214–47.
24 S. Dubnow, *Nationalism and History*, (New York: Atheneum, 1970), p. 129.
25 *Times*, 20 May 1989.
26 *Independent*, 19 september 1989.
27 The description is taken from an article by Jean-Charles Szurek, 'Le camp-musée d'Auschwitz', *Bulletin trimestriel de la Fondation Auschwitz*, No. 23, January-March 1990, pp. 9–34.

INDEX

Index

167

Index